JOURNEY
—to—
JESUS
WITH ME

JOURNEY *to* JESUS WITH ME

ROSE JACKSON-BEAVERS

All scriptures are taken from the King James Version of the Holy Bible.

Manufactured in the United States of America

Library of Congress Control Number: 2022951308

ISBN: 978-0-9753634-6-1 (Paperback)
ISBN: 978-0-9834860-8-4 (eBook)

Publication Date: January 2023

For information regarding discounts for bulk purchases, please contact Prioritybooks Publications at 1-314-306-2972 or rosbeav03@yahoo.com.

Other books by Rose Jackson-Beavers can be found on Amazon.com and Barnesandnoble.com

CONTENTS

Acknowledgements xi
Foreword xiii
Introduction xvii
My Journey to Jesus xxi

DAY 1 1
The Mourning/Moaning Bench

DAY 2 7
Understanding the Power of Prayer

DAY 3 15
Never Depart from God

DAY 4 23
Faith

DAY 5 31
It's About Being Faithful in Tithes and Offering

DAY 6 37
Waiting on Love

DAY 7 43
Changing Your Appearance

DAY 8 49
Are You Thankful?

DAY 9 57
Do You Trust in God?

DAY 10. 63
Aging is a Beautiful Thing

DAY 11 71
Blood is Thicker Than Water

DAY 12. 79
Birds of a Feather Flock Together

DAY 13. 87
Being Obedient for Heavenly Rewards

DAY 14. 95
Let Your Light Shine for God

DAY 15. 103
Am I My Brother's Keeper?

DAY 16. 109
Sharing the Good News About God Through Our Testimony

DAY 17. 115
Taking Care of Your Mind, Body, and Soul

DAY 18. 121
Does Prayer Change Things:

DAY 19. 129
Beauty Fades, but the Love in Your Heart Lasts

DAY 20. 137
A Different Time, A Different Day

DAY 21. 143
All Birds Do Not Flock Together

DAY 22. 149
The Lies You Tell

DAY 23. 155
Are you Compassionate?

DAY 24. 161
You Are What You Eat

DAY 25. 167
Watching Your Mouth

DAY 26. 173
Jealousy and Envy, the Thief that Steals

DAY 27. 179
Falling in Love with Jesus

DAY 28. 185
The Truth Shall Set You Free

DAY 29. 191
Waiting on God

DAY 30. 197
Thankful and Blessed

Final Words 205
Dedication 209

ACKNOWLEDGEMENTS

My husband, Cedric: You are a good man. I may not tell you that often, but you exhibit the principles and attitude God wants us to show others. Thank you for always sticking by me.

To Adeesha: Being your mom is the single best thing that has ever happened to me. I love you so much, and I'm thankful God allowed me to raise you. Continue to strive and never give up. Remember, your parents will always have your back.

To my only grandson: Gary Isaiah, there is so much joy and love around you. We are grateful to God for allowing us to witness your birth and life. We pray He will allow us to be in your life until you are a young man. We love you, our first grandson.

To all readers, to those who know God and want to know Him better, I pray this book will allow you to remember every time God showed up in your life.

To the late Connie Mae and LJ Booker: Without you both, I would not have pursued the things I love doing. I always had your blessings, and I appreciate you. You made sure we knew God, and I will always love you for that. Thanks for taking us to church and not just sending us, for it is the questions you answered for us after services that strengthened us in Jesus.

To all readers who email me, call me, or show up at events I present: Thank you so much. There is no way I could continue to write without readers pushing me on. Your support means the world to me.

To Shelia Bell: I love you for always supporting me and taking on my clients. Thank you for your editing services.

To Rosemary Jackson-Moore: I have joy because you are in my life. I don't know how God led you to me, but I am so happy He did. Thank you for editing, inspiring me, and being a part of my tribe.

To my siblings, Chester, Regina, Glorina, Johnaver and Charlotte: Thank you for your love and support. Also, for the good meals Glorina cooks to keep the family together.

Nikina and Kendrina, your laughs are contagious. To all my nieces and nephews, continue to strive for greatness always. Keep God in your life.

To Kendrina: Continue to lean on God. I promise He will hold you up. Remember, whatever you ask in Jesus' name, either He will do it, or His grace will be sufficient for you.

To effectively use this devotional is a simple process. I have allocated thirty (30) days for you to read and complete the exercises inside this book. Each day, read the Bible verse and devotional reading. Next, read the scriptures and surrounding scriptures in your Bible to better understand what you are reading. I have included personal stories about how God worked with, and helped, me in the same Bible verses. It was comforting to know that God brings us through so much. If you look closely at your life, you can see He has been working with you the entire time.

Complete the exercises and watch God work in your life to strengthen your relationship with Him. Finally, the exercises will show you how to help others so they too can have the experience of a lifetime. It will allow you and others to look at your past and future in getting closer to our Savior.

Thank you for taking this journey with me. I appreciate you all!

FOREWORD

National bestselling author, Shelia E. Bell

Writing, editing and publishing is such a tremendous blessing in my life. I have enjoyed a literary career that spans twenty-two years with no signs of me slowing down in sight. It is not often that people recognize and then walk in their true purpose and identity, so I am especially grateful to God for bestowing his favor, mercy and grace in and over my life, and giving me the drive to live this life and travel this journey. It has been, and remains, my ministry and my God-given gift.

Along my literary journey, I have been fortunate to meet a plethora of authors and readers but there are few who I have made a true connection and friendship. Author, entrepreneur, prayer warrior, and mental health facilitator Rose Jackson-Beavers is one who has made a positive, lasting impression in my life. When we initially met almost ten years ago our spirits connected right away. Her positive light shines bright in my life and in the lives of others. Rose's genre fiction books are entertaining and engaging and have garnered much recognition in the literary world. Moreso, her books, lectures, and conferences on the subject of mental health emphasize paying attention to this often neglected part of our health. Rose is passionate about imparting knowledge concerning the importance of seeking therapy and counseling, all which she discusses, shares and facilitates with hundreds of people at religious establishments, through her books, and at events across the country.

When Rose asked if I would write the foreword to "Journey to Jesus with Me" I was honored and extremely grateful. I immediately knew she did not make this request lightly. She is known to be a faithful, praying woman so I knew it was a request I had to give serious consideration. If God led Rose to ask me then after praying about it myself, I had to be obedient and do what God directed.

Reading the personal stories and testimonies shared in this devotional journal made me revisit my own childhood. Fortunately, my siblings and I experienced much of the same Godly teachings by my parents, and so I identify and connect with the author in many instances throughout this book.

It is a timely release, especially during such a time as this when the world seems to be in a state of chaos and unrest. Sadly, wars, poverty, famine, thirst, violence, and homelessness are prevalent. People are weary, people are angry, people are troubled, and many have gotten off their spiritual journey. Many have turned *from* instead of turned *toward* God, leaving their mental and spiritual state in disarray. We are in need of a message. We are in need of a return to the Word of God. We are in need of the teachings and testimonies such as those shared in "Journey to Jesus with Me." Our spirits need recharging and refueling.

"Journey to Jesus with Me" explores and uses various Bible scriptures and incorporates them into this devotional with the ability to reawaken our spirituality and remind us of the benefits we have when we are obedient toward God. It is a testament of the importance of the Bible scripture that instructs us to *train a child in the way he should go and when he is old he will not depart from it (Proverbs 22:6 paraphrased)*. I believe this book has the ability to lead those who have gotten off course back to God. The nuggets of wisdom, passages of scriptures, and being open and honest with her readers is what sets this devotional apart from others. If you dive deep into these pages and you are open and receptive, I am confident you will find a deeper, more satisfying relationship with God the Savior. If you do not know God, or you do not have a personal relationship with Him, or you have momentarily gotten off track, this devotional journal can be a source to revitalize your hope, reset your direction, and renew a right spirit within. May each reader and the author be blessed by the message in this book.

Shelia E. Bell
Author and Editor
God's Amazing Girl

INTRODUCTION

My mother was baptized at nine years old. Throughout her lifetime, she never once left the church. That means that when she was pregnant with me and each of my siblings, she remained in church. If I didn't know anything else, I knew my mom loved God with a solid conviction. She demonstrated this love in her daily prayer life, the way she loved and helped people, and the way she ensured that her kids knew Him.

In all honestly, she had no choice. Her father reared her and her siblings, who sang in a gospel quartet so, throughout her childhood they went to church and prayed often. Mom leaned on God as she had been taught daily, and when she was going through difficult times with her stepmother, God always came through. My mom left Itta Bena, Mississippi, at fifteen years old. Her dad had remarried, and her mom was not visiting her children often. My mom wrote her fraternal uncle telling him she was unhappy and that her stepmom was mentally abusing her. Although as Mom said, it was many years later when they heard the words, "mental and emotional abuse" and realized this is what they had experienced. My great uncle sent for mom, and she became a new resident of East St. Louis. My Uncle Herod was a staunch Christian. If you were in his house, you went to church under his wings. Mom attended his church, where she served in the choir and usher board. She also wrote plays and sang solos.

I don't ever recall a time she was not attending church or praying. My mother was a praying woman. If she strayed at any time in her life, she still stayed in church. That meant if she went dancing and stayed out until the wee hours of the morning, when my uncle pulled out in his car to go to church the following day, she was right there.

Connie was not perfect by a long shot. Like many other young people, she wanted to have fun, go on dates, and do whatever she wanted. Yet, even as she experienced things and sinned, Mom still prayed and asked God to forgive her. Not a perfect person, but she had a perfect desire to be like Jesus. How do I know? I watched my mom, went to church with her, was a part of all the plays she wrote, and studied lessons with her. Mom prayed with her children. I saw her struggle, fall, and get back up. Even in her struggles, she always called on God. Like her elders, she knew exactly who to call when she was in need.

My journey to God started in my mom's belly. Once I was born, she continued to take my siblings and me to church. If Mom left town, Dad made sure we arrived at the community church on time. Mom was not a member of the Methodist church because she was Baptist, but whenever she had to leave town, she didn't want us to miss going to church so our dad got us ready, and my brothers walked us the three blocks to church.

When I was six, my mom had to go out of town for a funeral. She laid our clothes out for church and combed our hair, but Dad had to comb my hair again by the time we were ready. I recall him brushing my hair up into a ponytail because it was so messy. My hair was stiff, and the ponytail stood straight up, but I proudly walked to church ready for Sunday school because that was what my mom taught me. Today, I still walk proudly into church because that is what I learned. Because of my teaching, I love God. I prayed daily for God to strengthen my walk and help me along this journey. So, please take this journey with me and let us do things that please our Lord.

This book is about how my mom kept us on the highway to Jesus. I created this activity book to strengthen our relationship and bring others with us on this journey. It is a guide with assignments designed to be completed at the end of each day. When completing the assignments, think about your situation and then meditate on what you wrote. Read the Bible verse and apply it to your life. Invite someone else on this journey by having them complete the daily activities also. Let us introduce as many people as we can to Jesus. Thank you for joining me.

MY JOURNEY TO JESUS

I have always been a praying woman. I cannot remember when it started because I've been in church all my life, and my mom taught us to pray and depend on God. My memory takes me back only so far. My earliest recollection of church is around four or five years old, standing in front of the church reciting my Easter prayer. I still remember it. I stood with my feet planted firmly against the carpeted floor, wringing my hands, and said, "What you are looking at me for, I just came to say, have a happy Easter Day."

My mom always dressed us up and put us in the front of the church, reciting poems or being in a play. We were always busy and active in learning about God. Mom taught us that we could trust God and have faith that He would provide our needs no matter what happened in our lives.

Over the years, I have found this to be true. I have seen God work miracles when others said it was impossible. I have seen money flowing through our house as a kid when mom complained about being broke and paying her last dollar to the church for tithes. I have seen people healed who doctors gave no chance to survive. I know God is real and that He is able. I trust in Him with everything in me and love him because He loves me.

Isn't that the way human beings are? When someone loves you, it is easy to love them back. For me, God has been a part of my life since I was old enough to talk or walk. As of this writing, I trust in Him even more as an adult. I have also taught my daughter about

God and to lean on Him. I don't know what I would do if I didn't know God. He is my source of life in every way. I am so grateful that my mom encouraged us to read the Bible and go to church. As a matter of fact, I am grateful that she took us to church and guided our learning experiences. And when we needed answers, she was well studied and found answers and helped us understand the meaning and what God expected out of us.

I hope through these thirty days of devotions and stories, you will be able to see when God saved you, or when you thought you were alone, how He carried you. I hope for those who are reading that you begin to search for your truth in God, and that you will find purpose and love for the Almighty. I hope you learn that you can call on Him when you need Him or when you want to say, "Thank you, Father, for loving me enough to save me."

I am so glad God loves me. I know that all of my blessings, health, and needs are provided because I know Him and Glorify Him, I will do so for the rest of my life.

DAY 1

Acts 2:38-39

Then Peter said to them, Repent and be baptized every one of you in the name of Jesus Christ for the remission of sins, and ye shall receive the gift of the Holy Ghost. For the promise is unto you and to your children, and to all that are afar off, even as many as the Lord our God shall call.

THE MOURNING/ MOANING BENCH

I loved attending church, seeing everyone, and learning all about God. My mother was a Christian and a long-time child of God. As long as she could remember, she had always had him in her life. Her parents made sure that she and her siblings knew God too. They all attended church together, read their Bibles, and learned to lean on God.

In those days, the early '40s and '50s, she never wavered from her relationship with God until her death. Though mom would be the first to say she slipped, she backslid but knew that she would never get too far from God or His protection. Due to her healthy Christian life, Connie (my mom) made sure her children were reared on God's commandments, and like her, we would have a close relationship with our Savior.

I asked Mom once, "Why do you love God so much?" My mom said, "Our young days were vibrant, funny, and challenging. There were 12 children, and my parents picked cotton to feed us. Although most of the kids helped, we were still poor. We needed a lot of things, like other poor people. But God provided all our needs."

Mom told me she gave her life to Christ at nine years old. She told me about the morning bench. Many things happened in the church to prepare you for salvation. Black Baptist churches used to have "moaning/morning/mourning benches." I'm not sure of the correct word because everyone pronounced it the same. Our primary Christian teaching taught us that we had to sit on that bench until we felt God's presence in our lives. Before you were saved and accepted for baptism, you had to sit on the morning bench. The morning bench was simply a bare wooden pew that stood in the front of the sanctuary. It was the first pew on the left side of our church.

As kids, we wondered who would be first to get the Holy Ghost or the spirit and asked to be baptized. My mom received the Holy Ghost at the age of nine. I was much older. I remember sitting on the pew, but I don't remember when I got off to give my life to Christ. I had to be around eleven years old when I left the morning bench because I was already baptized when we left the Baptist denomination. Since I was going to a different denomination, I was rebaptized into my new faith as a Seventh-day Adventist. To my knowledge, several of my siblings sat on the morning bench as well. I'm so glad that I had a praying mom. God has blessed me over and over again.

SOMETHING TO THINK ABOUT

Do you remember your Christian conversion experience?
_____
_____
_____
_____
_____

Did your church have a mourning or morning bench?
_____
_____
_____
_____
_____

What did you call it?
_____
_____
_____
_____
_____

Did you learn about God as a child? What was your earliest teaching?

_____

_____

_____

_____

_____

Who taught you about God and how to build a relationship with Him?

_____

_____

_____

_____

_____

What do you remember the most about learning about God?

_____

_____

_____

_____

_____

ASSIGNMENT FOR TODAY

Talk to someone about God today. Read a Bible verse to them. Discuss your conversion and tell them why it is essential to know God. Try this one, Acts **2:38-39,** or choose one you like.

Who did you call?
_____
_____
_____
_____

How did it go?
_____
_____
_____
_____

Will you continue to teach people about God?
_____
_____
_____
_____

DAY 2

1 Thessalonians 5:17

Pray without ceasing.

UNDERSTANDING THE POWER OF PRAYER

I was an adult when I understood the true power of prayer. When I was 18, I joined an evangelist team at my church after the pastor called for young people to work for him during the summer in Springfield, Illinois. A couple of my church friends and I decided it would be a good idea to participate. I wanted to witness and lead people to the new church he was starting.

We were to tell people about the good news of Jesus. Outside of going to church and being an active participant, I had never witnessed to others. Unless you count how I was living, I always tried to live the way I thought would make God proud of me. I did everything I could to follow His teaching and adhere to the Ten Commandments. Though frequently, I fell short, I still strived to live right. But being a young person, dating, and hanging out with my friends, I'm sure I sinned or lived against God's principles.

During that summer, we all had a good time getting to know each other and knocking on doors to share the good news about Jesus. We sang and walked as we scouted doors to knock on. We took turns going up to the porches and introducing ourselves.

The first couple of weeks went well. Every door we knocked on opened, and the residents allowed us to pray for them after telling them about our church and mission.

I remember passing one house, and a colossal sized Pitbull

jumped out at us. It scared us silly, but we didn't run. We each screamed, "Jesus." The dog backed up and laid down. Amazingly, the gigantic, dangerous dog laid down as if he were bowing.

My friends and I looked at each other and started walking and saying, "Thank you, Jesus. Thank you, Jesus."

That was the first time I had actually called out to God, and He immediately responded. It is something I have never forgotten. It strengthened me to be able to knock on many more doors to proclaim the love of God.

Calling out to God when I am in trouble is natural to me now. There have been times when I almost had a car accident, someone tried to run me off the road, or something happened that was terrifying, and I called out to God to save me, and He did. God has been my protector for so long that I don't go anywhere without Him. I'm always praying and asking God to protect me, my family, and friends. I also pray that God protects others.

SOMETHING TO THINK ABOUT

Have you ever called on God and witnessed his works immediately?

_____
_____
_____
_____
_____

What happened?

_____
_____
_____
_____

How did this event impact your faith?

_____
_____
_____
_____
_____

Do you trust that God will always respond when you need him?

_____

_____

_____

_____

_____

ASSIGNMENT FOR TODAY

Call someone and pray for them. Let them know that God loves them so much that He sent his only son down to earth to save them. Use this verse, John 3:16, and when you finish, ask them if you can pray for them.

Who did you call?

_____

_____

_____

_____

Did you feel comfortable?

_____

_____

_____

_____

Were they accepting of your call?

_____

_____

_____

_____

Will you continue to call people?

_____

_____

_____

_____

DAY 3

Proverbs 22:6

Train up a child in the way he should go: and when he is old, he will not depart from it.

NEVER DEPART FROM GOD

My mother made sure we were active in church. We attended church weekly. That meant we went to Bible classes, youth programs in the evening, participated in plays, and sang in the choir. We stayed at our church as young people. Even after officially entering adulthood, we continued worshipping, all except two of my oldest brothers. They didn't go too far from the principles Mom taught, but they lived outside the church's' teaching.

For instance, my oldest brother started drinking until it was too much. He explained that military life was difficult for him. To cope, he drank. My second eldest brother partied and hung out with the popular people. My brothers were extremely popular and often found themselves following their friends and their friends lagging behind them.

For years, my oldest brother was missing from the church. He stopped being a regular member and went to being an absent one at seventeen. He would show up to all of our surprise every blue moon.

One day, Mom, I, and about five other family members were sitting in church enjoying the service when my eldest brother walked in the door. I happened to look back and saw him. I touched my mom, and we all looked back as he scooted into the pew a couple of rows behind.

After that day, he showed up every week. What was so amazing was that he didn't have a car during this period because he had too many car accidents as a heavy drinker and couldn't get insurance. So, he walked about five miles to the church. He didn't call anyone, just walked. After church, he would ride to Mom's house with us for dinner.

He came to church for about three months before he started noticing his ear was itching deep down, and he couldn't scratch it. After going to an ear, nose, and throat doctor, he was diagnosed with throat cancer. He received the diagnosis in March. He died in Jesus in July of the same year. The thing that made us the happiest was that my brother took Bible classes and we read the Bible to him daily. Not only that, his doctors and everyone who saw him, would remark how he never released that Bible to their care. As a matter of fact, the doctor said that the surgery he needed only gave him a slight chance of recovery, and that they didn't want to chance it because he wanted to study the Bible. The surgery would prevent it. Plus, they felt that putting him to sleep would be even more dangerous because of how massive the tumor was in his throat.

My brother's trek back to God made us all remember that Bible verse (Proverbs 22:6), which says, "Train up a child in the way he should go: and when he is old, he will not depart from it." My brother was raised in the church, knew God, and was converted. He left the church building, but he never left God.

SOMETHING TO THINK ABOUT

What is your understanding of the Bible verse, "Train up a child in the way he should go: and even when he is old, he will not depart from it."

_____

_____

_____

_____

_____

Have you ever applied it to a time in your life when you left the church and returned?

_____

_____

_____

_____

_____

Do you believe parents should train up a child? If so, how?

_____

_____

_____

Are you applying this Bible verse to your life, your child, or grandchild(ren)? Why, or why not?

ASSIGNMENT FOR TODAY

Do you have a child, grandchild, niece, or nephew? If so, ask them if they know about God. Ask their parent(s) if it is okay to share about God with their children. Talk to the parent(s) as well. Do they know God? Let them know that God loves them. Answer any questions they may have. Remember, children always have questions. Be patient with them.

Did you share God with a child or their parent(s)?

_____

_____

_____

_____

Have you ever done this before?

_____

_____

_____

_____

Did it feel different due to the COVID pandemic?

_____

_____

_____

Do you feel like your conversation was helpful to the listener?

_____

_____

_____

_____

DAY 4

Matthew 21:22

And all things, whatsoever ye shall ask in prayer, believing, ye shall receive.

FAITH

I grew up in a household of ten people. This included eight children plus my mom and dad. You learn to have faith when you have that many people living under one roof. Everyone needed something. Dad was the only person working, so we had to rely on prayer to get the extra stuff we wanted.

Mom taught us to lean on God, pray when we needed things, and call on Him when we were in trouble. Those consistent church meetings and Christian activities were important in our spiritual growth. In addition to attending church, we studied the Bible and asked Mom plenty of questions. To us, our mom was a Bible scholar. This was due to the length of time she was in church. Her dad was a quartet singer and traveled all over the South, singing gospel songs. Mom was a converted nine-year-old who loved God. That meant that she had the Holy Ghost and gave God her life. Our mom wanted us to have the same Christian experience, so she passed all the learning and studying she did on to her children--all eight of us. Mostly she read the Bible and told us stories about Jesus.

It wasn't unusual for us to pray for extra stuff like cars, clothing, trips out of town, and other things that weren't in the budget. But because we were a praying family, God provided so much more. We were taught about faith and to believe, and we did.

When I was ready to be married, I talked to my oldest brother. "What should I look for in a husband?"

He responded: Check to see if he loves God. Ask him to go to church with you. If he does, then you know he cares. If he keeps on going, he loves you."

I prayed for a good husband. I prayed for a child. I prayed hard to have a good life, and I wanted a Christian husband.

When I started dating my husband, I asked him to go to church with me. The following week we went. He enjoyed himself and for the next 17 years, my husband continued to go to church with me. We have been married for 36 years, and though he does not go now, he is still a praying man and a good person. He helps the needy, our families, and donates to charities. He is not a problem but is a great father, an awesome granddad, and a loving husband. I prayed and asked God for what I wanted. I waited and believed that God would give me the desires of my heart, and He did. I'm so grateful that my mom taught us to pray, and to read and understand the Bible. More than anything, I am so glad my mom showed us that God would take care of us if we accepted Christ as our Savior and believed and had faith that He would do what He said he would do.

SOMETHING TO THINK ABOUT

Do you believe God will honor His word by giving us the things we ask for in prayer?

_____

_____

_____

_____

_____

Have you asked something from God and you didn't receive it? How did you feel? Did you feel like God didn't keep His word?

_____

_____

_____

_____

_____

Why do you think God wouldn't answer your request?

_____

_____

_____

Do you trust God enough to wait? Sometimes when we ask for something, it may not be what God wants us to have because He wants us to have greater than our request.

_____

_____

_____

_____

_____

How strong is your faith in God?

_____

_____

_____

_____

ASSIGNMENT FOR TODAY

If you have ever doubted God, share with someone how your faith changed in Him. Explain how you began to trust in God and have faith that he would do what he promised. What changed for you?

_____

_____

_____

_____

How did it feel to share your story of faith?

_____

_____

_____

_____

Do you feel it made a difference to the person you spoke to? Why or why not?

_____

_____

_____

_____

Will you share your story again?

_____

_____

_____

_____

DAY 5

Malachi 3:8

Will a man rob God? Yet ye have robbed me. But ye say, Wherein have we robbed thee? In tithes and offerings.

IT'S ABOUT BEING FAITHFUL IN TITHES AND OFFERING

I watched my mom lay out her bills and write checks to pay them. As I monitored the process, I noticed her getting a little frustrated. She said, "Money is going to be really tight this month."

Why, I thought? I tilted my head in her direction and looked at her quizzically. Finally, after watching her in deep concentration, I interrupted her. "So, Mom, why are things so tight?"

She looked up and explained. "The electric bill is higher, and this is the month for property taxes on the house in addition to water, gas, car insurance, and food. So yes, it's going to be difficult."

I pointed to the first check she wrote and asked, "Then why give the church money when you are trying to take care of home?" I must have been about 16 years old. So, my young mind thought, *Why help the church when we needed the help?* I couldn't conceptualize that. I believe you should take care of your home first.

"Mom put her ink pen down and explained. "I am paying tithes, which is an offering I give back to God for the blessings He's given us. The Bible said to return ten percent of your earnings to God and the storehouse. This money is used to maintain the church, pay bills, provide Bible classes to people, and pay the salaries of the pastors. When we give to the church, we are taking care of our home too. It's a place we go to worship, study, work with others, and become closer to God. When you return ten percent, which is all God requires, the blessings come back tenfold."

I stared at her. "Why would God want you to give away money and suffer?"

She explained it was about faith. "I believe God will provide when we have faith and believe in Him. Also, remember God always makes a way."

A week after our conversation, I heard Mom talking excitedly in the kitchen. I went in, and she was talking to my oldest brother. I heard her say, "The insurance company sent me back an overpayment that I had been paying for months." She waved her hands into the air. "Thank you, Jesus. This is more than I need."

She turned to me. "Rose, this is what I meant. I paid tithes to God first, and he returned them to me tenfold. So, I got more than what I needed. I had no idea this money would be coming, but God knows all. Be faithful in your tithes, and God will be faithful to you."

Another thing Mom said that day was, "If you don't pay God his ten percent, you will pay someone else. It is either Him or some other unexpected thing that will happen that will take that ten percent and, in some cases, more." I have seen people have car problems, phones turned off, higher bills, car repossession, and other things that are going to get that money. The Bible does say that when you don't pay tithes, your pockets will be like holes. It's happened to me before. So, I trust in God and pay my tithes, and he has never failed me.

Over the years, I have paid tithes, and often make donations to other non-profits for needy kids. There have been many times when I have paid 20 percent and sometimes more. It didn't go directly to the church, but it certainly went to help those in need. When I am faithful in giving tithes and offerings, God has been bountiful in blessing my family and me.

SOMETHING TO THINK ABOUT

What is your understanding about paying tithes and offering?

_____

_____

_____

_____

_____

Are you a faithful tither?

_____

_____

_____

_____

_____

Do you trust that if you are faithful in tithes that God will be faithful to you? Why or why not?

_____

_____

_____

_____

_____

What can you do to make sure you can set aside your tithes and still pay your bills?

_____

_____

_____

_____

_____

ASSIGNMENT FOR TODAY

This week set aside and tithe a little more than what you usually tithe. Share if you get a return on your blessing.

Did anything out of the ordinary happen? For example, did you receive a raise, find money in another purse or pocket, or receive another blessing?

_____

_____

_____

_____

Do you expect that when you give more, more will come back to you?

_____

_____

_____

_____

How does it feel to give to the church or to pay your tithes?

_____

_____

_____

_____

DAY 6

Proverbs 18:22

Whoso findeth a wife findeth a good thing, and obtaineth favour of the LORD.

WAITING ON LOVE

It takes a lot of prayer and patience to wait on God to send you your soul mate. When I was growing up, most of my friends and family members looked forward to the day they would find true love and get married. It was normal to want a husband, kids, and a white house with a white picket fence. My friends and I chatted about this all the time. If we were dating someone, we naturally hoped they were the man that God had chosen for us. Unfortunately, or fortunately, depending on how you want to say it, they were not the man we prayed for or the man God chose for us to spend our lives with. For most of us, later we wiped our foreheads with gratitude.

I was raised during a time when people believed in marriage and the expectation was that if you prayed and waited God would send you your soul mate. Often though, we would fall for the guy that was not God's choice for us. When things fell apart, we would pray that God would either heal our heart, send the right one, or remove the one who was causing us problems or broken hearts. Then we would sulk at the way we had been treated, and sometimes take our pain out on the next person.

My mom would tell us to allow God to send our soulmates. She encouraged us to be patient and pray, asking God to allow us to recognize him when he came. So, Mom would tell us about Proverbs 18:22, but she would also tell us not to sit and wait. She would say, "go to school, work, date, but pray." If the person was not a good person, or did not treat you right, you knew that was not who God sent.

I did what most girls did. I prayed, dated, and got hurt by guys who meant me no good. When I was in pain, I ditched the guy and vowed to wait next time. When I finally waited in earnest, God sent me the person. I knew it the day I met him. He met my best friend first. She wasn't attracted to him and sent him over to meet me. She actually introduced us. We were young and having fun. I had recently broken up with an older guy who was a teacher, so I wasn't looking for anyone. I resigned myself to remain single.

When my future husband asked me to dance, I did. We sat at the table and talked. At the end of the evening, I gave him my phone number upon request. When I returned home that night, I told my thirteen-year-old brother a guy would be calling but I didn't want to speak to him. When he asked why, I said, "Because I am not ready to get married and that is the man I am going to marry." I don't know how I knew, but I felt God's hands on it.

Thirty-eight years later, I still believe that when I stopped trying to find me a man, it allowed God to send who He had chosen. I also recognized it was from God and since I was still suffering from the loss of the man who was not from God, had decided I wasn't interested in dating again. Thankfully, I finally opened my eyes in time to see a blessing coming into my life. Thanks to my husband who had found a good thing, and my little brother who had kept being a pest and giving me the phone after I asked him not to, we are still happily together.

SOMETHING TO THINK ABOUT

What do you think about Proverbs 18:22?

_____

_____

_____

_____

_____

Do you believe that if you pray for a good husband God will send him?

_____

_____

_____

_____

_____

Why is it so hard for women to wait on the man God has for us?

_____

_____

_____

_____

_____

Do you believe God has created someone just for us?
_____
_____

Are you married?
_____
_____

Do you believe he is your soul mate, the man God created for you?
_____
_____
_____
_____

Are you willing to wait on God, or do you think you can find a husband on your own?
_____
_____

What do you think about the dating scene now?
_____
_____
_____

ASSIGNMENT FOR TODAY

If you are single, write a prayer to God. Tell him what kind of spouse you desire. Tell Him you will have faith and wait. Be honest and talk to your father. Be consistent, pray often about it, and be patient.

Are you willing or strong enough to wait on God?

_____

_____

_____

_____

Can you resist temptation? If not, ask God for help. Add this to your prayer.

_____

_____

_____

_____

_____

_____

_____

_____

DAY 7

Exodus 20:4

Thou shalt not make unto thee any graven image, or any likeness *of anything* that *is* in heaven above, or that *is* in the earth beneath, or that *is* in the water under the earth."

CHANGING YOUR APPEARANCE

When I was about thirteen, I asked my mom if I could have surgery to correct my nose. I was upset that my brother teased me about the size of my nose and often called me names. I was so frustrated that I wondered if my parents could afford plastic surgery so I could have one like I had been hearing a lot about from famous people. My mom refused to entertain such nonsense.

Around my sixteenth birthday, I brought the plastic surgery topic back up to my mom. I told her that I hated my nose and pleaded with her to find the money to pay for it. Again, my mom tried to speak some positivity into my life by explaining that God made me, and I should be happy with God's design because he didn't make any junk. That didn't stop me. I wanted to be beautiful, and my nose was stopping me. I remember my mom reciting a quote that said, "Lord help me to accept the things I cannot change, change the things I can, and the wisdom to know the difference (R. Niebuhr)." She reiterated that I was beautiful and that the only person who was bothered by my nose was me and that my brother loved me. Mom said she had spoken to my brother, and he would not tease me about my nose again. Then she asked, "How do I look to you? How do your aunts look to you?" I told her I thought she and my aunts were beautiful. Mom said if she and her sisters were beautiful with their noses why didn't I think I was beautiful with mine, since I had the same nose as they did. She further reminded me that my brother had a big nose so when he teased me then he was also talking about himself. She asked if I thought he was ugly. Of course, I told her *no* and that everyone thinks he is handsome. Mom took my hand into hers and said, "You look just like him. So, if he is handsome, then you are beautiful. You two have the same nose."

That day I learned two things. I learned about Exodus 20:4. We had been reciting it at church for years before divine services started, but now I knew the meaning. I realized that we were made in God's image and that I was beautiful because God didn't make junk. I realized I idolized famous people from watching TV and thinking that what I saw was the image of natural beauty.

God does not want us to idolize anyone other than Him because he is a jealous God. I learned that day from a simple quote that I should be happy with who I am. Mom told me if I want to change, change my attitude, or the way I treat others and leave what God made perfect alone.

SOMETHING TO THINK ABOUT

Have you ever felt like you were not beautiful? Why?

_____

_____

_____

_____

Did you seek to change your appearance? Is it something you would need to have surgery to alter?

_____

_____

_____

_____

If you needed surgery to change your appearance but you did not have the surgery, what stopped you?

_____

_____

_____

_____

Are you happy with your appearance?

_____
_____
_____
_____
_____

What can you do to feel better about yourself?

_____
_____
_____
_____
_____

What does Exodus 20:4 mean to you?

_____
_____
_____
_____
_____

ASSIGNMENT FOR TODAY

Look in the mirror. Tell yourself you are beautiful. List your qualities. Repeat them while you are looking into the mirror. Believe what you are saying. Throughout the day, keep telling yourself you are special, and that God doesn't make anything that isn't beautiful.

How does it feel to affirm to yourself that you are beautiful?

_____

_____

_____

_____

Will you continue to speak positive affirmations to yourself?

_____

_____

_____

_____

Practice doing this daily until you no longer have to affirm it because you *know* it.

_____

_____

_____

DAY 8

Psalm 107:1

O give thanks unto the LORD, for *he is* good: For his mercy *endureth* forever.

ARE YOU THANKFUL?

I found myself feeling inferior to other successful businesswomen because I read about all the things they were doing to make money. I felt like I wasn't doing enough and did not have the visibility to attract more business. The social media platform can be challenging to one's self-esteem if you are not careful. Daily, sometimes frequently throughout the day, I would jump on social media to see what was going on. I noticed nothing but ads on Facebook and Instagram. These ads were from people in like businesses and emphasized making you a millionaire or telling you how to create a platform to attract more customers and get paid. Everything was one big ad. The worst thing about it was everyone was saying the same thing. I asked myself, *Do they all go through the same training?*

As I watched and read about all these so-called millionaires and ingested their stories of success, it occurred to me that these same people who had me all bothered, almost made me miss my blessings. Hearing about their successes and their businesses blinded me to the fact that I was blessed beyond means. I forgot that these same people were looking for and bragging about the success I enjoyed. I realized I was already where they hoped to be. Not only that, I was also totally debt free. God had blessed me and my husband tremendously and through his blessings, my life was so bountiful that I was blessing many others. Why did I forget that God had been so good to me and my family? Why was I feeling so unsuccessful?

I realized why. I had failed to say daily to God and others how appreciative I was of all my blessings. God knew I was thankful. I had said it plenty of times, but I did it in prayer. I didn't speak it out loud because I didn't want to feel like I was bragging. I kept my blessings secret with only a few people understanding my worth. So, while everyone was all out front, I hid.

We are supposed to testify about God's blessings and let people know God keeps His word, that He is an awesome provider. There was nothing wrong with saying out loud that God has blessed me and my family. No, I don't have to brag, I don't have to make up lies, or try to hustle money out of people. But I can thank God and let others know about His promises and how God blesses us when we live according to His will. You are supposed to share your good news and lead others to Christ. There is nothing to be ashamed about in doing that!

SOMETHING TO THINK ABOUT

How do you measure your success? By your bank account, fame or something else?

_____

_____

_____

_____

_____

Are you where you want to be in this life?

_____

_____

_____

_____

_____

How often do you give thanks to God?

_____

_____

_____

_____

_____

How do you share the good news that Jesus saves and God indeed provides?

_____

_____

_____

_____

Do you feel like you are bragging or drawing people to Christ when you share the good news of Him keeping his promises?

_____

_____

_____

_____

ASSIGNMENT FOR TODAY

Walk around your home and touch everything in each room while giving thanks to God for blessing you and your family.

How did it feel?

_____

_____

_____

_____

Did you realize you had so much?

_____

_____

_____

_____

Are your blessings overflowing to the point you believe you have too much?

_____

_____

_____

_____

How do you feel realizing how blessed you truly are to have a bed to sleep in, a couch to sit on, lights to turn on, etc.?

_____

_____

_____

_____

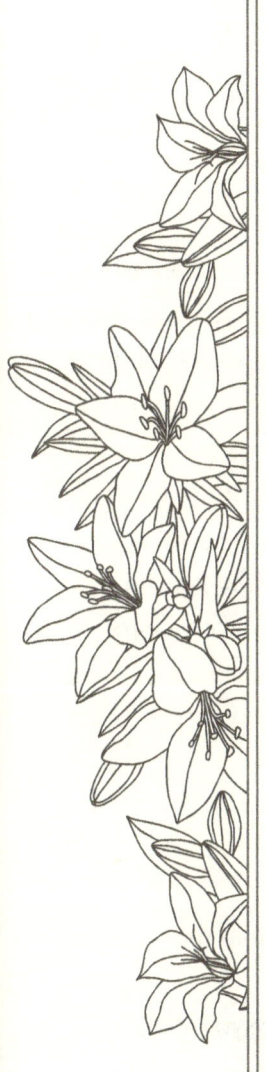

DAY 9

2 Samuel 22:3

The God of my rock; in him will I trust: he is my shield, and the horn of my salvation, my high tower, and my refuge, My saviour; thou savest me from violence.

DO YOU TRUST IN GOD?

My siblings and I sat in awe, listening to our mom tell us the story about how trusting in God saved her. Mom had left the house near dusk to pick up some Chinese food from a local restaurant. The restaurant was on the very popular State Street where buses and cars are a constant. As she returned from picking up her order, someone approached her from the back and said, "Get in your car and do not turn around!" She said she felt something shoved into her back and a man said, "I have a gun and I said get into your car." He said his words carefully, with a burst of anger, in a low-hoarse voice.

"No. I will not get into the car." Mom stood steadfast with her feet planted into the ground.

He shoved the gun deeper into the center of her back. "I said, get into the car. Now!"

"I said, I am not getting into anything."

"Don't make me kill you right here, lady. Get into the car right now." He shoved her hard.

Mom said she bowed her head and prayed. "Are you leaving me now, Lord? I trust you to protect me." She said she waited. "Lord, surround me with your angels."

Suddenly, Mom said the man took off running so fast as if someone was chasing him. She thanked God for covering her.

"Mom, were you scared?" we asked, as we sat back biting on our lips and fingers. I thought, *What if he had taken Mom somewhere and we never heard from her again?*

"I was not afraid. I trusted God. I knew if I got into that car, he could take me away and I would never be heard from again. I trusted God and believed He was covering me, so I was not afraid."

One thing I loved about my mom was that she had an unbreakable trust in God. I think of that story all the time, but I also have my own stories of times when I knew that if I had not trusted God, I could have caused myself to have a heart attack out of fear. Every story Mom shared about her trust in God and how it always turned out for the best, increased my belief that God was my rock and my shield and would protect me. I loved hearing her tell her stories, but what I loved the most was learning about the power of God and His protection, if I only believed.

SOMETHING TO THINK ABOUT

Do you trust in God?

_____
_____
_____
_____
_____

Has there ever been a time in your life when you felt you needed God and He was not there?

_____
_____
_____
_____
_____

How did you feel?

_____
_____
_____
_____

Did God not showing up shake your faith?

_____

_____

_____

_____

_____

Think of a time when you needed God to show up. Did He?

_____

_____

_____

_____

_____

ASSIGNMENT FOR TODAY

Go to a quiet part of your house where you can think about God and pray. Close your eyes. Think about a time you were in fear for your life. Maybe you were almost in a car accident or almost tripped and fell. Maybe you were pulled back by a stranger from walking in front of a car while talking on your cell phone. What role did God play? Do you see where He protected you from danger or harm?

_____

_____

_____

_____

_____

_____

_____

_____

_____

_____

_____

_____

_____

_____

DAY 10

Psalm 71:9

Cast me not off in the time of old age; Forsake me not when my strength faileth.

AGING IS A BEAUTIFUL THING

My mother died when she was 78 years old. Before her death, she worried a lot about being able to care for herself. Her biggest concern was being a burden to others. While she worried about aging and her independence, we worried about losing her.

I like to say my mom was a Bible scholar because she knew so much about the scriptures. Often, I would ask her questions about what God thought about our time on Earth. She would say that in Psalms 90:10, He says, "The days of our years are threescore years and ten…" Mom explained that was seventy years because scores meant twenty; she felt that we had seventy years on Earth. Mom would say anything over that was a bonus.

My mom loved living. She loved people, but more than anything she loved talking about God and the Bible. I would call to ask questions and to have her tell me Bible stories. To me, she was the original storyteller in our family.

There was one thing about my mom that I noted. She didn't want to become an old woman. Old to her meant feeble, not able to walk around or move like she wanted to. She feared not being able to care for herself, and did not want people to be burdened. She always said, "When someone has to change my bottom or feed me, that will be my time to go to God. I don't want to be a burden to anyone. When my work is completed, or I can no longer function, I pray that God takes me.

I hated hearing her talk like that. I didn't want to lose my mother under any circumstances. Her family needed her, regardless of her ability. But as Mom became feeble and unable to care for herself, we witnessed a sadness in her eyes that was hard to miss. Even knowing her feelings about being a burden, our hearts did not want her to leave. We told her over and over that we would care for her as she did for us, without regrets or attitudes.

Mother was a beautiful person. For as long as she could, she served God and lived her life like it was golden. But as she hit age 70, she began to have back problems, could not stand for long periods of time, and was on a walker. She did not like that, but she managed. The older she became, she began to inform us about her desire not to be a burden. Still though, we explained she wouldn't be that to us.

I secretly thought Mom was afraid of aging. Years later, I began to see what she meant about being a burden. At age 77 she began to deteriorate after being diagnosed with cancer. She went through radiation. After her last treatment, she became very ill and was rushed to the hospital. She stayed in the hospital for over thirty days before she eventually came home. We saw improvement, but then she became weaker. Mom's entire family - immediate and extended - stayed by her side for months caring and praying for her. But in her eyes, there was a longing to go home safely to her Father in Heaven.

My mom was blessed with bonus years. She loved life and appreciated the aging process until she could no longer care for herself. When she became feeble, she felt comfortable being in the arms of God. My mother loved God, and she was sure she would be with Him. But still, we had not abandoned or cast her aside. We gave her assurance that we would be there until the end, and we were.

My family rotated taking care of our mom. We sang and prayed her right into the bosom of our Lord. Aging is a beautiful thing when you are with people you love and they hold your hands until you are no more. Aging is also a beautiful thing when you have completed your assignment on Earth, and you are ready to see your Heavenly Father.

SOMETHING TO THINK ABOUT

How do you feel about getting old?

_____

_____

_____

_____

_____

Are you worried that no one will care for you?

_____

_____

_____

_____

_____

Do you think aging means you will become feeble and unable to care for yourself?

_____

_____

_____

_____

Do you have plans for who will care for you when you become too old or feeble to take care of yourself?

_____

_____

_____

_____

Will you be ready to see God when your work is completed on Earth?

_____

_____

_____

How have you prepared yourself to see God?

_____

_____

_____

_____

Do you think aging is a beautiful thing?

_____

_____

_____

ASSIGNMENT FOR TODAY

Write down your plans so your family will know what your desires are should you become unable to share that with them. Let your children know what they need to do and where essential papers are such as insurance. Put a plan in place for your family.

_____
_____
_____
_____
_____

Where did you place your important papers?

_____
_____
_____
_____

Who will you leave in charge?

_____
_____
_____
_____

Have you talked to your family?

_____

_____

_____

_____

DAY 11

Deuteronomy 6:7

...and thou shalt teach them diligently unto thy children, and shalt talk of them when thou sittest in thine house, and when thou walkest by the way, and when thou liest down, and when thou risest up.

BLOOD IS THICKER THAN WATER

There were only a few issues that made my mom angry when we were growing up. They were when she caught her children arguing, lying, or gossiping. But mom had one thing that she reminded us about constantly, and that was the quote, "Blood is thicker than water." I'm not sure what age I was when I first heard her say that, but it was before I was ten.

My mother wanted her children to bond, protect each other, and live as close to God as possible. Growing up in a family with eight kids and a mom and dad was hard. Though we loved each other, sometimes dealing with the issues of families like, *who took my ink pen, someone ate my sandwich,* or *he pushed me* rattled my mom's nerves. It was partly because if we were arguing, then that meant we hadn't learned any of the things she was teaching us.

We spent many hours in church. We attended Bible classes, worship services, and the young people programs in the evening. Some of us were in the choir. That was another two to three hours of practice once a week. Mom used to plan activities for us to ensure that we were learning about God. We would read the Bible, have song services, and she would tell us Bible stories. In the only way she knew how, she was teaching us about God. After all, mom didn't learn how to be a mom through experiences with her mother. She was self-taught. There were times when we would see her sitting quietly in a corner reading huge books on Psychology or how-to books on motherhood. We also knew she saw a therapist for further support.

If mom heard us fighting and screaming at each other, it would hurt her feelings. "Didn't I teach you all to respect and love each other? I'm not going to always be around, and you will have to look after each other." She would explain to the boys that they were leaders and had to protect their sisters, not tease them. Still, one of the four boys would continue to chase and tease us mercilessly. The girls didn't tease the boys, but we argued with each other about clothes, using the phone, and over hair products. But still, the four girls were good friends. We loved all our siblings. Mom's teaching taught us to love, respect, and support each other.

The quote mom drummed into our heads about how blood was thicker than water was a lesson she taught us because she wanted us to stay together as a family and have strong positive relationships with each other and with God.

As I see my family and witness our closeness, it is clear that the lessons my mom taught her eight kids was a lesson we embraced and followed into adulthood. My siblings and I are very close. We talk to each other as much as we possibly can, although we live in different cities. Our love for each other runs deep and nothing can separate us from our childhood instructions to love each other, read the Bible, and stay in prayer with God. In our family, we believe that blood is thicker than water, and to us, water meant all those influences that could pull us apart from our family and God.

SOMETHING TO THINK ABOUT

Have you ever heard the phrase, "Blood is thicker than water?"

_____
_____
_____
_____
_____

What does it mean to you?

_____
_____
_____
_____
_____

What does God expect of us concerning our family(ies)?

_____
_____
_____
_____
_____

Are you teaching your loved ones about building a relationship with each other and with God?

What does your family think about you as a Christian?

What can you teach your children, siblings, or friends about God?

ASSIGNMENT FOR TODAY

Call five people in your family. They could be siblings, nieces, nephews, aunts, or any relatives who need to know more about God. Invite them to church and volunteer to pick them up. If they say no, keep inviting them until they say yes. Don't give up!

Who did you call?

_____

_____

_____

_____

How did they receive your invitation?

_____

_____

_____

_____

Will you try to call them again?

_____

_____

_____

_____

Did you call another person?

_____

_____

_____

_____

DAY 12

Romans 12:2

And be not conformed to this world: but be ye transformed by the renewing of your mind, that ye may prove what *is* that good, and acceptable, and perfect, will of God.

BIRDS OF A FEATHER FLOCK TOGETHER

At age ten, I met a girl who would later become my friend. We lived in the same area, maybe a few blocks apart, across the main street. We met while walking down the street. I don't know where either of us were walking to, but we were cordial to each other. We stopped, introduced ourselves, and shared important information like where we lived, who our family members were, and where we went to school.

Through this chance meeting, we discovered that my brother was dating her sister. We were ten years old at the time, so they had to be about 15. We became fast friends. When my mom found out I was walking at least five blocks to see this new friend and that sometimes my friend was doing the same thing, Mom stopped it. Mom thought it was too dangerous for me to cross the major street and forbade me to see her again. I cried and asked her why. I had told Mom who her family members were and told her about my friend's sister was dating one of my brothers.

"Why can't I see her again? She's my best friend." Mom said I had just met the girl and it was also because of my friend's sister. Mom thought her sister was too fast, meaning hot in the pants, sneaking to see my brother, and if she was doing that, maybe the little girl was like her sister. I got mad. My mother said she didn't want me walking around and away from the neighborhood. She wanted me to be more, to grow up and become a doctor or something. She said I had to choose friends wisely. I told Mom my friend was brilliant. Years later, she did very well in corporate America.

What I understand now is this: My mother wanted me to hang with people who were like me. I was a bookworm. I read everything I could find from newspapers to encyclopedias to dictionaries. I was such a voracious reader that when I ran out of good material to read, I read stuff I had no business—like grown-up books. Mom wanted all of her children to be associated with Christians and people working toward success. Like-minded people were who she hoped her children would want to play with or invite to church. She later learned that my friend was like me, a bookworm too.

God wants the same thing for us. He doesn't want us hanging with people who will sway us from Him, but He does want us to bring people to Him. God does not want us to conform to the world, do harmful things, or participate in worldly activities. He wants us to be in the world, but not of the world. We should not conform and accept sin and those that sway us from God. We should put our minds on good and acceptable things.

My mom wanted the same for her children. In her way of communicating, she would use quotes and adages to explain stuff to us. If that didn't work, she went to her trusted Bible. "Birds of a feather flock together" was something she always said, but she was clear that flocks could have lousy behavior or good. She wanted assurance that we would know the difference between the birds in the world and choose wisely those who would help us stay closer to God.

SOMETHING TO THINK ABOUT

What do you think the following Bible verse means? And be not conformed to this world: but be ye transformed by the renewing of your mind, that ye may prove what *is* that good, and acceptable, and perfect, will of God. (Romans 12:2).

_____

_____

_____

_____

Do you believe that all birds of a feather flock together? Why or why not?

_____

_____

_____

_____

Apply this adage to your childhood. Who did you hang out with as a young adult? Did they represent success or failure? Did they bring you closer to God?

_____

_____

_____

_____

How do you determine if you are participating in activities that are of the world?

_____

_____

_____

_____

Do you know how to step away from those things that could sway your mind from the things God wants you to do?

_____

_____

_____

_____

What do you tell your children about selecting friends? How do you select who you will be around?

_____

_____

_____

_____

ASSIGNMENT FOR TODAY

It is said that, "You are the average of the five people you spend the most time with." This quote is attributed most often to motivational speaker, Jim Rohn. The impact of this statement can reach further. Studies show that we are not only influenced by our friends, but our friend's friends and so on. How people can influence you should be a major concern. I understand why my mom was so specific about who she wanted her children to surround themselves with because the impact of who we were, and who we could become in the future, was something she didn't take lightly.

What my mom was trying to say is who you spend the most time with can impact your future. She wanted us to examine our circle of friends and to see how they were influencing our behavior. She was so particular about how we spent our time and who we shared it with because she wanted us to excel. She believed we would be less likely to achieve our goals if we were hanging with folks who didn't have achievement on their minds. So, what my mom could not eloquently say was that we are not just the average of five people; we were the average of all the people who surrounded us.

Look at the people you hang out with. Who are they?

_____

_____

_____

_____

_____

Do you all enjoy the same activities?
_____
_____
_____
_____

Do you have similar goals?
_____
_____
_____
_____

Are you all seeking Christ as your Savior?
_____
_____
_____
_____

Are you volunteering to help others?
_____
_____
_____
_____

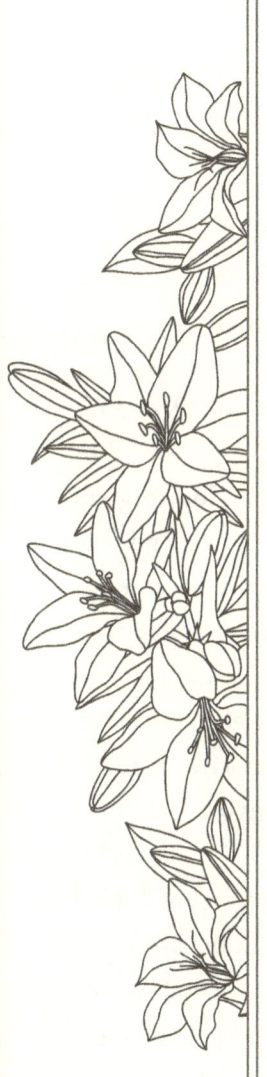

DAY 13

Exodus 20:12

Honour thy father and thy mother: that thy days may be long upon the land which the LORD thy God giveth thee.

BEING OBEDIENT FOR HEAVENLY REWARDS

I have to admit that when I learned Exodus 20:12 about honoring thy father and thy mother, I felt safe. I believed by following God's commandments, He would ensure that I would live long. Loving my parents was easy to do. Why? Because God blessed me with wonderful parents.

My mother wanted to be a mother. She asked God to grant her the skills she needed. She ordered Psychology books and read as much as she could on parenting. Mom said it was because her mother was not a solid presence in her life. She stated that her stepmom was a horrible person and had she stayed, she would not have retained the Christian principles she learned as a girl. Her uncle from the Midwest sent for her after receiving a long letter from her about the treatment she and her siblings were receiving from their dad's second wife.

After arriving in East St. Louis, Mom's relationship with God grew stronger because she had to attend church with her uncle and his family. Mom continued to follow the commandments as she understood them. She would pass down her love for God and Bible stories to her children.

We grew up learning the Bible and being active in church. I knew the Ten Commandments. I always felt that God would accept me into his kingdom with open arms if I followed them. I also loved my parents. I knew that whatever I had in this life I would share with them. They did everything they could to provide for us and train us up as God wanted us to go, based on Biblical principles. I vowed to return everything they gave to us and more.

When my parents became ill, I was there for them. Dad was the first to become seriously ill. Whatever he needed, my husband and I were on it. I spent so much time with him, taking him to lunch, doctor appointments, shopping, to Mom's house, and I would sit on the porch with him. My nephew became his primary caretaker, but I was there as much as I could. I saw my dad at least three days a week and enjoyed every minute of it.

I did the same with my mom. Again, my nephew became the primary caregiver, and I came four or five days a week to make sure she was well taken care of. I also wanted to hear her tell me more Bible stories. She was so good at it and knew them well.

My parents adopted my nephew and two of his siblings due to some family issues. We would talk about the caretaking responsibilities and how well we coordinated the activities with each other and some of our other siblings. We were proud because we had done what the Bible said about honoring our parents.

Did we do it so God would reward us with a long and good life so He would honor his promise to us? No, we did it out of love for the beautiful parents He had given us.

I have to admit, there are days I become disappointed because I have arthritis, and it is painful. I have prayed and asked God why I have certain ailments. I thought I did what He required. Then I remember that everything God promises is not about this world. Some things are for after I die. I am just grateful I was blessed with the parents God allowed me to have. There is nothing I wouldn't have done to make them comfortable and happy, while feeling safe with their loved ones. To me, this is what God expects of us - to love our parents as He loves us. He loved us so much that He sent His son to this sinful world to die for us and save us. Our honor should also extend to God, for it is His love that keeps us.

SOMETHING TO THINK ABOUT

Who would take care of your mom and/or dad should they become ill?

_____

_____

_____

_____

_____

Do you and your family have a plan?

_____

_____

_____

_____

_____

Do you study the Bible regularly to learn what God's expectations are for you and your family?

_____

_____

_____

_____

How do you feel about the commandment to honor your mother and father that your days on this Earth may be long?

_____
_____
_____
_____
_____

Are you looking forward to Heaven? If you are, how are you preparing for it?

_____
_____
_____
_____
_____

Would you do whatever it takes to care for your parents, like quit your job, or move them in with you? Why or why not?

_____
_____
_____
_____

ASSIGNMENT FOR TODAY

If you are not the only child, schedule a phone call, Zoom, or face-to-face meeting with your siblings to discuss your parents' care should they become ill. Who will be the primary caretaker? Who will stay with them? If they live in separate households, how will you handle this?

_____

_____

_____

_____

_____

Do you have a plan? If you do not have a plan, create a plan for either your care, your parents, or a sibling who may become ill. The best plan is to plan early. If you have to make changes you can.

_____

_____

_____

_____

_____

_____

DAY 14

Matthew 5:16

Let your light so shine before men, that they may see your good works, and glorify your Father which is in heaven.

LET YOUR LIGHT SHINE FOR GOD

I remember the day clearly. I had attended my twenty-year class reunion a day earlier. Upon returning to the office the next day, I showed my staff, and others in the lunchroom, pictures from the event. My senior high school class was large but intimate. Over the years, we mostly remained in contact through emails, social media, and bowling parties to raise money for the class.

The twentieth reunion was special. Many of our old and new friends, and those we hadn't seen for years, registered to attend the events. We were all excited. One of the speakers was a girl I knew well and had shared a couple of classes with. We had also become published authors who started publishing companies to help authors from our city.

I enjoyed the speakers and all the weekend activities. As I was proudly sharing the many pictures I had taken, more than 50 percent of those who viewed the pictures picked out the speaker and said, "She is a Christian."

I stared at her picture. What did they see in her that they didn't see in me? After all, they didn't say I was a Christian. I was on some of the pictures with her as well. I asked, "Why do you say she is a Christian?"

One of my staff said, "Look at her. It's all over her face." I took a long look. She didn't have on make-up and she wore no jewelry.

On her head was a beautiful, puffy afro. She looked beautiful. I was thinking, *do they say she is a Christian because she was clean-cut and clean-faced?*

I searched my co-workers' faces for their answers. One said, "You can tell she's a Christian. It's all over her body."

I was disappointed. Why couldn't the employees of the agency I worked at see that I was a Christian? I loved God. I wanted people to see the light in me too. I just closed down. I stopped talking and felt defeated. Later that evening, I called my mom. I told her what had happened and asked her why they didn't see that I was a Christian?"

My mom listened before she repeated the verse back and explained what it meant. "The young lady is doing good works for the glory of God. She is teaching, preaching, and I'm sure from what you have said that she has no problem with glorifying God. She is allowing her work/light to shine for God. She's not afraid to share the goodness of God. She is allowing her light to shine toward people who may be in the dark about God."

I listened. I understood what my mother was saying. I love God. I've known Him all of my life. I couldn't imagine Him not being the head of my life, but the truth is, I had been trained in many of my supervisor's classes not to talk about God, politics, or salary issues on the job. I have always been in management, so we could not discuss religion in the office due to the potential for lawsuits. It is a sensitive subject. Everyone may have different beliefs and may be sensitive or feel that you are discriminating against them if they expect you to have an issue with their religion. Religious discrimination is illegal under Title VII. The law prohibits religious harassment of employees or making offensive remarks about a person's religious beliefs or practices, so I learned to refrain from discussing this topic.

Even though I couldn't discuss it openly, I tried to let people see my heart. I was a good person. Still, we must remember to share the good news about God. When we share God's goodness, people will see the light in our works.

SOMETHING TO THINK ABOUT

How do you display your light for Jesus?

_____
_____
_____
_____
_____

Do you think Christians should hide their work for Jesus in fear of persecution?

_____
_____
_____
_____
_____

Do you believe that Jesus is the only spiritual Light in the world and that you can spread His light to others? If so, how do you spread it?

_____
_____
_____
_____

How will you get the spiritual Light?

_____

_____

_____

_____

ASSIGNMENT FOR TODAY

If you can, send a flower or plant to an elderly person. If you need to, take it to them. Preferably, pick some fresh flowers or buy a Bible and take it to someone who might not own one. Invite someone to brunch or lunch and let them feel your genuine love for God, them, and others.

_____

_____

_____

Is there an old friend, neighbor, or church member you have not seen or talked to in a while? If you have a church member who is missing from attending church, call and invite them to lunch and let them know you have been thinking about them.

_____

_____

_____

_____

DAY 15

Exodus 20:15

Thou shalt not steal.

AM I MY BROTHER'S KEEPER?

As a young boy in the 1970s, my brother, Sylvester, was a paperboy with his own paper route. He made good money riding around on his bike throwing papers in people's yards. He saved his money to spend on his parents and siblings. I still remember some of the gifts he bought us with his savings. He was such a good brother. Sylvester was my mom's second oldest and second boy. He was responsible and wanted to make his own money. He was kind and respectful. His customers loved him. Our local newspaper featured him in the paper when he was thirteen.

One day while he was out tossing papers, Sylvester found a wallet along the sidewalk. He brought it straight to our momma. Mom called the police and they came to get the wallet. They contacted Mom later to tell her the man had received his wallet. Later, the man came to our house and thanked my brother and gave him ten dollars. He gave each of us four girls one dollar each. My other brothers were upset. One of them said, "Sylvester gave him back six hundred dollars; they could have given him more money for his honesty."

On the other hand, Mom was happy because she said she had taught Sylvester correctly, and he wouldn't have taken something that did not belong to him. We had been in church all our lives. Mom had taught us the Ten Commandments. She said as long as we followed them, we would all see each other again. She stressed to us not to lie but to always tell the truth. She told us that if we practiced lying, we would steal, and we could end up breaking another commandment, *thou shall not kill.*

My siblings and I practiced living the commandments. She taught us to look after our brothers and if something didn't belong to us to give it back. Two of my siblings ended up doing things outside of God's commandments, but it had to do with substance use. Mom used to say, "I taught you all to be your brother's keeper, and even though two strayed from God and later returned, they never hurt anyone but themselves. Thank God they returned to church and God. They fell back on their love for God."

SOMETHING TO THINK ABOUT

Did your parents or guardians teach you the Ten Commandments?

_____

_____

_____

_____

_____

Would you have returned the wallet?

_____

_____

_____

_____

_____

Would you have expected the man to give you something more for your honesty?

_____

_____

_____

_____

_____

What do you teach your children or other family members about stealing?

_____

_____

_____

_____

_____

ASSIGNMENT FOR TODAY

If you hear a good story about someone doing a good deed, let them know they are appreciated and that what they have done is admirable. If you do not know anyone who has done an honorable deed, pray for all people to act according to God's standards. Write your prayer down and use it to pray for people regularly.

_____

_____

_____

_____

_____

_____

_____

DAY 16

1 Chronicles 16:8

Give thanks unto the LORD, call upon his name, make known his deeds among the people.

SHARING THE GOOD NEWS ABOUT GOD THROUGH OUR TESTIMONY

This is my testimony. God has blessed me in so many ways. I can honestly not remember ever having to go without anything in my life. Whenever I needed anything, my parents made it happen. When I was old enough to work, I bought what I wanted. I prayed for a God-fearing, good man and God blessed me with a good husband. He is a saver. He is always trying to make sure we are doing well financially. With God's hand on our lives, I am very humbled.

We have not been selfish with our blessings. We have shared with others until we felt we were hindering their growth. Our parents did not have to want for anything. If we had it, so did they.

I always heard others openly telling people about their tremendous blessings. I was not too fond of that. It felt too much like bragging. One day, I was talking to a co-worker who was sharing with me, and others, how God had blessed her with a new car and home. I shuddered at her telling so much of her business.

One day, after she shared more good news, I said to her, "Why do you tell people about what God is giving you as a blessing? You must be careful. People are envious. Some might want to do you harm."

She responded, "How else would people know how God blesses me? I want them to know that God loves them too, and if they love Him, He will bless them too." She further said, "Not only will I share about my blessings to others, but I will also scream out about God's goodness."

I was a little embarrassed that I hadn't felt that way. I learned a lot that day. I learned that we should share the good news about God, His blessings, and His love for us. If people don't know about our loving God, why will they want to follow Him?

It is important to spread the good news about God's love, mercy, and goodness. When we have a testimony, God expects us to share it. People need to hear our testimony, because our testimony might help bring others to God. He is faithful to us. Let us be faithful to our loving Father.

SOMETHING TO THINK ABOUT

What do you think it means to testify?

_____

_____

_____

_____

_____

Do you have a testimony? Is it about your finances, health, or spiritual?

_____

_____

_____

_____

_____

Are you willing to share the good news about Jesus Christ?

_____

_____

_____

_____

_____

Tell us how good God has been to you.

_____

_____

_____

_____

_____

What are you praying and asking God to do for you?

_____

_____

_____

_____

ASSIGNMENT FOR TODAY

Share your testimony about God's goodness. Don't you have a story to share? Did God wake you up this morning? Do you have food, a job, bills paid, and a roof over your head? Once you share about your blessings with others, ask them to tell you how God has blessed them.

_____

_____

_____

_____

_____

_____

_____

_____

_____

_____

_____

_____

_____

_____

DAY 17

Proverbs 19:20

Hear counsel, and receive instruction, that thou mayest be wise in thy latter end.

TAKING CARE OF YOUR MIND, BODY, AND SOUL

I was between the age of ten and twelve years old when my mom packed us four girls into her Buick Sedan and took us to visit her therapist. Mom had eight children, but she took just us girls on this particular day. The psychiatrist wanted to meet her children. I am sure the older boys did not want to go.

Mom had been talking about us, and the therapist wanted to see who these children were that had their mom wrapped around their fingers. You see, my mom lived and breathed for her children. She had given up a lot of her youth to raise her brothers and sisters and now her children. Having eight children, all stairsteps in ages could be for many, quite difficult.

Mom was a reader. She read everything she could to learn about motherhood. She wanted to understand the best ways to care for herself and her family. She wanted assurance she was being a good mom, which is partly why she was seeing a therapist. After watching the *Young and Restless* soap opera television show and witnessing the characters bragging about their therapists, Mom said, "If they can see someone, so can I." She had a healthy perception of taking care of her mind, body, and soul.

As a young person, I watched and listened. Therefore, I grew up with a strong perception of self-care and the importance of having a healthy mind. Because of my experiences with meeting a therapist before my 13th birthday, I did not hesitate to seek help when I needed some mental support.

I believe what Mom said, which was never fear getting help when you need it. If you need to talk to someone, see a therapist. When you have aches and pain, you see a medical doctor. Keeping the mind healthy is just as important as keeping all the other organs of our body healthy. People should understand they are not crazy when considering seeing a therapist. God wants us to be healthy mentally, physically, and spiritually. It's okay not to be okay. So, take care of the body God gave you. Remember, a wise man seeks counsel.

SOMETHING TO THINK ABOUT

How do you feel about counseling or seeing a therapist?

_____

_____

_____

_____

_____

Have you, or someone you know, sought therapy?

_____

_____

_____

_____

_____

Do you think God would disapprove of you going to others for counsel?

_____

_____

_____

_____

_____

How can you change the stigma of mental health in your family or community?

_____

_____

_____

_____

_____

ASSIGNMENT FOR TODAY

Do you know someone who may have lost a loved one? Do you know someone who is feeling sad or suffering from anxiety? If so, pick up the phone or get in the car and go visit them. Listen to their concerns or their pain. If needed, share the national hotline number for them to get professional counseling. Let them know there is nothing wrong with seeking help. Share Proverbs 19:20: A wise man seeks counsel. Remind them God wants us to be healthy.

DAY 18

Mark 11:24

Therefore I say unto you, What things soever ye desire, when ye pray, believe that ye receive them, and ye shall have them.

DOES PRAYER CHANGE THINGS:

Prayer does change things. I smile when I think of something my mom said a few months before she died. Mom had been sick for about four months. To us, it was sudden because we didn't expect her to die. But Mom told us to get her things in order because she was soon to go home. She started reminding us where important papers like insurance, bank and deed information, etc. were, so we would be prepared when the day came for her to die in Jesus. But, like most children, we didn't want to hear that a parent would soon leave us.

When Mom was diagnosed with small cell lung cancer, we were all shocked, including Mom. Mom did not smoke. The doctor said she had stage 2. She underwent chemotherapy at age 78. Three weeks after finishing her treatment and ringing the bell, Mom became gravely ill. She was in the hospital for about 40 days.

Her children, church family, siblings, and friends prayed hard for her. Finally, I remember her coming home and lying in her bed with a big frown. I asked, "Mom, what is wrong?" She said, "I would be gone, but you all prayed me back." I laughed, not at her, but at how the power of prayer gave us more time with her.

This is not the only time I have seen prayer change things. All my life, I watched Mom pray for things such as financial blessings, or for her car to get needed repairs to prevent it from breaking down on the highways. I was with her once when the car was having difficulty staying running, and when we arrived home, it stopped in the driveway. I can hear Mom praying and thanking God for getting us home safely. Five years ago, that happened to my family and me while driving with serious car problems from Aurora, Illinois, which was about three hours from our destination. We prayed all the way home. Once inside the garage, the SUV stopped. We were so thankful God heard us and protected us when we called on Him.

I do not doubt that prayer changes things. My dad rarely took days off from work. At vacation time, he would take the pay instead so we could have an overflow. Vacation pay always gave him extra money to buy clothes and shoes for eight growing bodies. He enjoyed his job, so if he had to take off for a family funeral, it would be for no more than two days. One time, when Dad was sick on a Sunday and was near tears, I started praying. He worked on Saturdays but not on Sundays. He worked for himself and also for a large company as a welder. On this day, I watched him holding his jowl in so much pain. There was no way he could make it until the next day. I started praying. I called different dentists to see if someone could see him as an emergency. The pain of having this toothache was etched into his face. I will never forget it.

After calling about ten dentists in the phone book and praying, I reached an answering service. I explained how much pain my dad was in, pleading for them to help him. His face was swollen and had begun to reshape itself. The person who answered the service said she would relay the message, but that the office was closed, and if needed he should go to the emergency room. I hung up and prayed again. I knew the hospital would not pull the tooth or make it all better. After praying, a dentist returned the call. He had my mom bring dad to the office on his day off, gave him antibiotics, and did whatever else he did to stop the pain and bring down the swelling. Dad was relieved of the pain, went to work that Monday, and eventually the doctor pulled his tooth. I was so happy the dentist went in on his day off because of the cries of a teenager worried about her dad. I know it was the hand of God working. Again, God showed me that prayer changes things. In fact, I believe prayer changes everything.

SOMETHING TO THINK ABOUT

How often do you pray to God?

_____
_____
_____
_____
_____

Do you trust God and believe He will answer your prayers?

_____
_____
_____
_____
_____

If you have children, what are you teaching them about prayer?

_____
_____
_____
_____
_____

Have you introduced your friends, family, or others to the power of prayer?

_____

_____

_____

_____

_____

ASSIGNMENT FOR TODAY

Nurture a shared prayer life. Spend more time today in prayer. You can do this by sharing your testimony and praying for others. Some ways to do this can include:

Calling a friend and letting them know you are praying for them and that you are always available for prayer. Ask if they want you to pray with them.

_____

_____

_____

_____

_____

_____

_____

_____

_____

_____

_____

_____

_____

_____

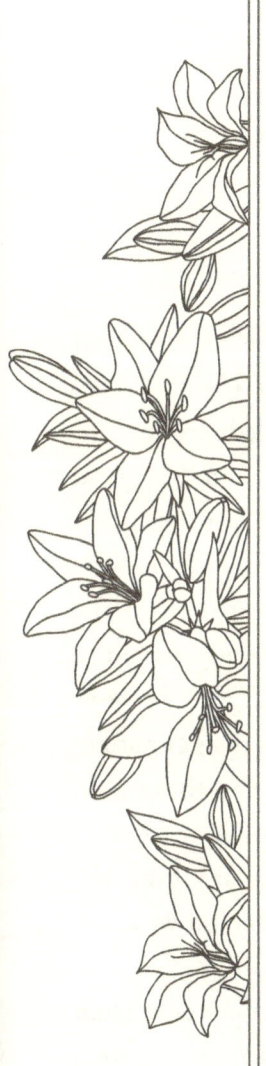

DAY 19

Proverbs 31:30

Favour is deceitful, and beauty is vain: but a woman that feareth the LORD, she shall be praised.

BEAUTY FADES, BUT THE LOVE IN YOUR HEART LASTS

It is better to be beautiful on the inside than out. You can always change the outside. Beauty fades, but a heart of gold lasts a lifetime. This was a lesson often drilled into me and my siblings. Our mother prayed to God to help her to be a good mother. She loved taking care of her children and spent countless hours teaching us how to be good people. Part of her lessons were about the heart and being a good person that treated others the way we wanted to be treated. Because of her strong teachings, my siblings and I grew up with a good concept of who we were. There were times when we would fall off due to images put before us that made us feel less than we were. When that would happen, Mom would sit us down at the kitchen table and talk to us. She was a good communicator, but more than anything, she was very open. No subject was off limits with her, and we asked everything.

The question always came up about who was the prettiest. Mom would tell people all her children were pretty, each of us having beautiful spirits and hearts of gold. I cannot ever recall her saying anything negative. On the contrary, she had one positive thing to say about each of us. Although, I didn't always like some of the descriptions she used to make us feel good about ourselves, I knew she was doing her best.

When people asked about us, Mom stood tall and proudly informed others about our strong points. There were times, however, when I would rather have one of the other descriptors she used for my other sisters. For me, she would say, "This is my smart daughter. She is good in her books and can wash clothes. Her whites are the whitest you've ever seen." Then she would say another sister was a great cook and decorator; another was her China doll, dressed well, and was so cute. She always said positive stuff but sometimes I wanted to be the cute one and not the smart one. When I would mention it, Mom would tell me that beauty is in the eye of the beholder. She would explain that each of us had our own concept of what was beautiful and what may be beautiful to one person, may not be beautiful to the next person. She further explained that we should all seek to have a beautiful heart. The inside was most important.

Mom said all her children were beautiful, but it was the smartness that she was most proud of about me. She felt I embodied intelligence that would get me further in life than just being cute. Mom said each of her children had unique abilities that would move them further in life. She was right. My sister, the great cook, eventually opened a barbeque stand that was very popular for the time she remained in business. My cute sister, the China Doll became a successful salesperson in make-up, dressing people as a personal shopper. She was the number one salesperson in many of her pursuits. She also served 14 years in the military. Mom wanted us to be focused on our hearts and spirituality. She said that we should look at the works people did, like what they did to help others, or how they treated their family and friends. Do they love God? That's what she wanted more than anything. She reminded us that beauty fades, but the heart could continue to grow and love.

That's how God wants us to be. He doesn't want us to focus on our outside beauty. He wants us to have a beautiful heart that loves Him and His children everywhere.

SOMETHING TO THINK ABOUT

What are your best attributes?

_____

_____

_____

_____

What's more important to you, the inside or your outside?

_____

_____

_____

_____

How do you treat people?

_____

_____

_____

_____

Do you think God would be proud of you? Why or why not?

_____

_____

_____

_____

_____

Would God be happy with you for how you treat yourself and others? Why or why not?

_____

_____

_____

_____

_____

ASSIGNMENT FOR TODAY

Stand in front of a mirror and search your face. What do you like the most? Your eyes, eyelashes, nose, lips? What part of your face makes you feel secure? Think about your heart. Do you treat people who look different than you better or worse? Do you treat people who are attractive better? Do you treat people with a heart of gold like they are precious? If not, what are the attributes people have that dictate how well you treat them or even respect who they are? Say a prayer. Ask God to help you treat yourself and others the way God expects you to. Pray often that God helps you to be kind to all people no matter the appearance or how they act. Your heart, your works, and keeping God's will is what He will judge us on.

DAY 20

John 14:23

Jesus answered and said unto him, If a man love me, he will keep my words: and my Father will love him, and we will come unto him, and make our abode with him.

A DIFFERENT TIME, A DIFFERENT DAY

When I was a teenager, I didn't want anyone to know that I loved God and regularly attended church. I kept my relationship secret because I didn't want people to laugh or bully me. When you are young, you tend to do dumb things, and I was no different from most teens.

I have been in church my entire life. Because of Jesus, I never experienced a lot of pain, heartbreak and did not ever recall lacking for anything. Yet, I was reluctant to share my God with anyone.

Many times in our youth, we are insecure. We want to hang with the in-crowd and we tend to hide behind our real persona. We naturally navigate to what is fun, popular, and what made us feel less conspicuous about who we were, or how others perceived us based on what was popular at the time.

My mother was an all-out front Christian mom, who didn't care who she offended. When she talked about Christ, she flaunted her relationship with Him. Others would listen and smile at her stories. It was so embarrassing for her children that she spent so much time talking about a person you couldn't see. It's not that we didn't honor or love God, but the truth is, He wasn't right there in our faces—He was in our hearts. That's where we kept him. This is what I realized as I became an adult. I understood that God had always been faithful in our lives. He kept us healed, healthy, and financially secure.

These are the reasons why my mother shared her proudest moments about God with others.

When I think of how Mom raised us, I smile. We couldn't visit new friends or people we didn't know well. Mom would take us to meet the family and see how they lived. Did they drink, have a bunch of men around, and were they Christians? The only way you would get to know or hang with her children was for you to go through her and my family. That's what this Bible verse says to me. If you want to see God, you have to love and follow Jesus. No one can get to Heaven without following Jesus. My mother said, "if you want to have a relationship with my children, you have to meet me and follow my rules." Are you developing a relationship with Jesus?

SOMETHING TO THINK ABOUT

How do you share the Word of God with others?

_____
_____
_____
_____
_____

Are you comfortable letting people know that you are a Christian?

_____
_____
_____
_____

How do you choose friends for you and your children? Do your children's friends have to come through you before you allow your children to go to their homes or attend activities away from you?

_____
_____
_____
_____

Are you open to learning more about God by reading His Word daily?

_____

_____

_____

_____

_____

ASSIGNMENT FOR TODAY

Tell someone today what it means to love God. Talk about what God has done for you and your family. Is there a particular blessing you want to share? For the next several days, tell people about a blessing you received. Let them know God loves them and that you want to tell them how good He has been to you. The goal is to become comfortable talking about God. How else can we share His blessings so that others will want to experience the same kind of love for Him?

_____

_____

_____

_____

_____

_____

_____

_____

_____

_____

_____

_____

DAY 21

1 John 2:15

Love not the world, neither the things that are in the world. If any man love the world, the love of the Father is not in him.

ALL BIRDS DO NOT FLOCK TOGETHER

Growing up can be a hard thing for young people. It can be hard not to succumb to peer pressure. The teen years are when young people want to be accepted, especially by those teens who are considered popular, cool, and who have it all together. Unfortunately, to be one of the popular people, you sometimes have to participate in activities that are not becoming of a Christian. This is a period when parents most worry about their children taking drugs, cursing in order to be accepted by others, and fighting to show they support their bullying friends. After all, some teens participate in things they know are wrong just to be accepted. For many young people it is better to be in the group than to be on the outside, being ignored or bullied, wishing they could fit in. For the young person that is trying to live for God, these are some critical times.

When I was in fifth grade, I met a young person who would become a lifelong friend. We spent all our young years together and attended college as roommates and even better friends. But there was a time my mom didn't want me to hang out with her. It was because of her sister's behavior at that time. Mom caught her with my oldest brother and told her on several occasions not to return but each time, she would sneak back over.

My mother believed all birds flock together. It was the one thing

I recall her telling us all the time that I didn't agree on. "Stay away from so and so, or you will get in trouble with them." A lot of times, she was right, but in this case, she wasn't. My friend was brilliant and was from a good family. Mom should not have judged my friend by her sister's character. Ultimately, Mom admitted she judged that person's future incorrectly.

I noticed that birds *do* fly together. I watch them all the time flying in formation, going to their next warm place. If we want to live for God, we cannot be of the world. We cannot straddle the fence with one leg hanging on the side of good and the other on the side of evil. We must detour from the negative V-formation and find our way to God. We have to show our love for God by doing those things that please Him and introduce others to Him. We cannot love both sin and God. We have to let one go. Who will you love and live for and stop straddling the fence of good and evil? Do you love God enough to stop partaking in this sinful world? Pray and ask God to help you. Just like He did it for me, I know He will do it for you.

SOMETHING TO THINK ABOUT

Who are you living for, God or the world of sin?

_____
_____
_____
_____
_____

Do you think you can enjoy the sinful fruits of the world and still live for God? Why?

_____
_____
_____
_____
_____

What kind of friends do you hang with? Are they Christians or living contrary to the Bible's principles?

_____
_____
_____
_____

Do you think you can go to parties, drink, curse, and do things that people say are fun and still glorify God to others?

What can you do to stop straddling the fence of good and evil?

Have you decided to follow Jesus?

ASSIGNMENT FOR TODAY

Call a friend. Invite them to join you on a prayer line or do a Bible study together. Are you comfortable doing that? Look at your friends. Do they love Jesus? If you cannot call them to discuss the Bible or Jesus, pray and ask God to help you share the word of God with them. If your friends do not love God the way you do, stop and pray for them today.

DAY 22

Exodus 20:16

Thou shalt not bear false witness against thy neighbour.

THE LIES YOU TELL

Growing up can be challenging, primarily when you have been taught right from wrong. But what happens when one parent is teaching their children to live by certain principles and the other one uses them to benefit him or herself.

My mother told us on many occasions not to lie, but to be truthful, and that as long as we practiced being honest when lied on by others, the truth would prevail. I have always tried to live by the adage, "the truth matters." Yet, I know many people who practice lying. These people lie so much that when they tell the truth, no one will believe them. That's the danger of lying.

People use lies to get out of trouble and sometimes try to get a better step up in life, like promotions and listing things they didn't do and making up things to say they did. The truth is, they know they haven't had the life experiences they listed. Yet, many people believe that a little white lie won't hurt others. This is not true, especially if it causes one to lose their job or to end up in jail.

My father was a hard worker, but he was a quiet man who didn't like to be bothered at home. He worked two jobs, leaving home at 4:00 a.m. to go weld for a part-time job. He would leave that job and at 6:30 he reported to his full-time job as a mechanic. He worked hard to take care of his large family. When his customers could not wait and interrupted him at home, he would ask his children to lie to the caller and tell them he was not at home.

Unfortunately, for my dad, my brother didn't like lying so when instructed to say he was not home, my brother gleefully stated, "My dad said he's not here." After that admission my brother was not asked to lie again. When I answered the calls, I began to ask one hundred questions like, "What is this call about?" "Why didn't you wait until he was at work?" and so many other questions until Dad didn't want any of us to answer his calls.

Mom told Dad he was teaching us to lie. Dad would say, "It's only a little white lie." Mom would say, "But those lies get bigger and worse and how can you get mad at the kids for lying when you are teaching them to do it?"

Dad stopped asking us to lie for him. He either answered the phone himself or just let it ring. Kids are like sponges; you cannot teach them how to do wrong things and become disappointed when they become experts at doing whatever you taught them. The Bible states we are not to bear false witness. In our everyday Bible lessons, we are taught not to lie. Make no mistake, you should not lie on anyone, including your neighbor, friend, or foe. Lying destroys reputations, honor, income, self-esteem, and so much more. It is much easier to follow the Ten Commandment that tells us not to bear false witness. You should not want to know how it feels to be on the opposite side of people lying on you.

SOMETHING TO THINK ABOUT

What do you think about the Bible verse, Exodus 20:16? Do you understand what it means to bear false witness?

_____
_____
_____
_____
_____

Have you ever told a little white lie?

_____
_____
_____
_____
_____

How did it effect you or the person it was told on?

_____
_____
_____
_____

Do you think it's ever okay to lie?

_____

_____

_____

_____

What will you teach your child or grandchildren about lying?

_____

_____

_____

_____

ASSIGNMENT FOR TODAY

Think about a lie you have told in the past. It could be from any time period in your life. What was the lie? Did it hurt you? If the lie was about a person, how did it affect them? Share your experience with your child or grandchild. Let them know that God is not pleased when we lie. Let them know how much lying can hurt others.

_____

_____

_____

_____

_____

_____

_____

_____

_____

_____

_____

_____

_____

_____

DAY 23

Psalms 145:8

The LORD is gracious, and full of compassion; slow to anger, and of great mercy.

ARE YOU COMPASSIONATE?

The Bible speaks about God's compassion and how He is slow to anger. Don't we all want to be that way? I wanted to and I was—I couldn't help it. I found myself wanting to help everyone. Even though I found myself being sympathetic to so many people, I couldn't understand why my mother was so kindhearted. I couldn't see that I was much like her in this area. I felt like people were taking advantage of her concern and her gentle spirit.

I wanted her to stop going out of her way to be so kind because I believed that people were using her for financial means and taking what they could get from her. Mom didn't seem to care, but I couldn't deal with it. Many times, I would stop her. "Don't give that person money, let them go to social services," I would say. Or I would tell her, "Stop letting people trick you out of things." Mom would smile and still help whenever she could.

One day, she explained not everyone is trying to take advantage of people. She further stated that God had her and that when she helped others, God was pleased because He was a compassionate God. Still, I wanted my mom to be careful. I mandated that she send people to me if she couldn't say *no*. Then the unthinkable happened. I realized I was worse than my mother. I could barely say, "No." I was so empathetic for others that I was giving away everything, until my husband stopped me. I am my mother. It was so hard not to help when God had blessed me abundantly.

To accommodate people, I began to send them to agencies that could help. I told them about jobs and other services that could put them back on track. If they refused, then I knew they were simply looking for a handout.

Being compassionate can mean spending time with people, helping them find services for their families, taking someone or inviting them to church, and teaching them about God. It doesn't have to be in the form of material things. God wants us to be compassionate toward others and help them have better lives. He wants us to be kind and lead people to Him, but we must be slow to anger, especially when we believe others are taking advantage of our kindness. When we are slow to anger, it can help keep us from getting into trouble. We prevent our anger from escalating and causing us to harm others, whether it is physically or mentally. Still, we can assist God's people by helping them find resources. God will be pleased.

SOMETHING TO THINK ABOUT

How compassionate are you?
_____
_____
_____
_____
_____

Are you willing to help others even when you believe they are taking advantage of you?
_____
_____
_____
_____
_____

What can you do to be more compassionate and supportive of others?
_____
_____
_____
_____

Are you slow to anger?

_____

_____

_____

_____

_____

When was the last time you became so angry you couldn't think straight? What happened and how did you handle it?

_____

_____

_____

_____

_____

ASSIGNMENT FOR TODAY

Call a food pantry, or if your church operates one, volunteer to serve. There are many agencies who give to the needy and who can really use your help. Volunteer for one day, or a few hours, and see how it feels to help others in need.

_____

_____

_____

_____

_____

_____

_____

_____

_____

_____

_____

_____

_____

_____

DAY 24

Proverbs 23:7

For as he thinketh in his heart, so *is* he: Eat and drink, saith he to thee; but his heart *is* not with thee.

YOU ARE WHAT YOU EAT

I have heard people saying things that reveal loud and clear that they do not have confidence in themselves. They predict failure and believe success for them is nothing but closed doors. Things like, "I cannot do that," or, "I cannot think straight," or, "I will never graduate," or, "I will never find a spouse."

I asked these self-doubters why they think so poorly of themselves and their abilities. Don't you know that whatever you put your mind to do, you can achieve it? What I usually hear is them telling me I don't understand, or they cannot do whatever it is. It is a belief that what we believe in our hearts comes out in our efforts. So, if you believe you cannot do something, then you are in fact, willing your mind not to act.

In this Bible verse, Proverbs 23:7 it says the same thing: that whatever a man thinks, so is he. We should remember what comes out of our mouths and what we believe can be detrimental to our well-being. Are we what we think? To me, if you think it, it's in you.

Proverbs 23:7 reads as if it refers to a man and his food. Is the man stingy? Does he want to share? It said, *eat and drink, but his heart is not with thee.* Is the verse saying to share even though the person doesn't want to? As I think about this verse, it makes me think that we are what we eat. In retrospect, it is true. When we overeat, many of us gain weight. When I put it into context with watching people and listening to the words coming out of their mouths, this could indicate that we are what we eat.

If we feed ourselves with a daily dose of self-doubt, words that don't inspire, and let those words marinate in our hearts and souls, yes, we would become those things. But what happens when you fill your mind, heart, and soul with positive affirmations, words of encouragement, and a healthy dose of self-esteem? Maybe then we could become extraordinary people.

You are what you eat. Stop stuffing your mouth and mind with negative-filled words and phrases that pack your body to complete fullness with fatty foods. These undesirable substances will only destroy your confidence and love for yourself. Eat positive words and watch your life begin to change for the better.

SOMETHING TO THINK ABOUT

What does this Bible verse mean to you?
_____
_____
_____
_____
_____

What do you think about yourself? Are you happy or sad?
_____
_____
_____
_____
_____

Do you believe you can accomplish anything you set your mind to do?
_____
_____
_____
_____
_____

Do you believe you are the sum of what you think about yourself? If so, and you have a negative concept about who you are or what you can become, how can you change that impression?

_____

_____

_____

_____

_____

If you have a positive image of who you are, how can you share it with others?

_____

_____

_____

_____

_____

What do you believe God's purpose is for your life? Does it align with how you feel or what you are doing today?

_____

_____

_____

_____

ASSIGNMENT FOR TODAY

Look in the mirror. Tell yourself you are beautiful, intelligent, and can do all great things with God on your side. Every day, stand in the mirror and give yourself positive self-talk. Repeat these words daily: "I am great. I am beautiful. I am talented. I can do all things with God's help."

DAY 25

Psalms 19:14

Let the words of my mouth, and the meditation of my heart, be acceptable in thy sight, O LORD, my strength, and my redeemer.

WATCHING YOUR MOUTH

Growing up, I sang in the young adult church choir. One of my favorite songs was made from the verse, Psalms 19:14. I sang that chorus with gusto. I wanted the words I used to be acceptable in God's sight. For many years, I never used words that hurt others, or said curse words. That changed when I became an adult. No, cuss words were *not* a part of my daily language, unless that is, if you made me angry. Not just angry, but *real* angry. When that happened, I didn't know what would come out of my mouth. My siblings would say, "that is not you," or, "I can't believe that came out of your mouth." My husband would look at me, disappointed.

Why was it so shocking to people that I could be taken to a place that was so unlike me? It was because I didn't use words that hurt others. In fact, I never did anything to affect others negatively. My whole life has been that of a servant helper. So, who was this girl that cussed when you took her there? She was *me*, the young woman who loved God. The young woman who didn't know how to control her anger. It was because it didn't happen often. I didn't know that it came from within me until my mom told me about her mother and her very lively vocabulary.

After talking to Mom, I tempered my words. To do that, I wouldn't let folks take me there. When and if they do, I pray. It's something I monitor daily, and I pray about it often. It is not a daily thing or even weekly. I am not perfect, but I continue to try to let the words from my mouth be acceptable in God's sight. I try to watch the words that come out of my mouth. I realize we are all works in progress, but prayer changes things. Daily, I pray that God will continue to work with me.

SOMETHING TO THINK ABOUT

What are some areas of concern you have and you know they need changing?

_____

_____

_____

_____

_____

Are you a work in progress?

_____

_____

_____

_____

_____

How has God delivered you?

_____

_____

_____

_____

Do you use words that are not appropriate?

If so, how are you working to change that?

ASSIGNMENT FOR TODAY

Pay attention to the language you use. Are all the words appropriate? Write down words you said this week that are not acceptable to God. Did you use a lot of inappropriate words? Write down a prayer to God and try to remember it. Recite it every time you say a word that is not like God.

DAY 26

Proverbs 14:30

A sound heart *is* the life of the flesh: but envy the rottenness of the bones.

JEALOUSY AND ENVY, THE THIEF THAT STEALS

It's easy to forget all your blessings when you are watching others receive things you want. I have never been a person that was envious of others. I've always been blessed to have great parents and siblings that I love and get along well with, for the most part. As a young teenager, I was allowed to drive my mom's new cars, and had several at my disposal. When I wanted and asked for new things, my parents made a way for me to get what I wanted. When I married in my twenties, nothing changed but my address. I just doubled the blessings.

As I matured and desired other things, not materialistic, I had all I wanted. I had nice cars, a home with no mortgage, money, and Jesus. But if you spend time on social media and watch the lives of others, you can begin to think that your life is so-so. Why aren't you traveling the world? Why aren't you meeting with hundreds of book clubs? Where are the thousands of readers who salivate to read your stories? But the latest crave is why aren't filmmakers knocking my door down? I'm a good writer. This is what looking at other folks' success can do to you. It can make you jealous when you should be proud.

But being envious is different. In Proverbs 14:30, it reads, "A sound heart *is* the life of the flesh: but envy the rottenness of the bones." I have never felt that kind of envy of others where it caused me to hate or want to hurt someone. Yes, I can say I want to be a successful, well-known author, and sometimes I feel a tad bit jealous of those who are, but wishing them harm, that's not me. if you are not careful, I do believe jealousy can turn to envy. To keep from feeling that kind of ugliness, I pray a lot. I also support those who are successful, even when I know they are not doing the same for me. But it is because of God's blessings in my life that I give back to others without allowing jealousy or envy to consume me. I am happy with what God has done, and will continue to do, for me. I'm grateful I know what being envious of others can do to the spirit, mind, and heart, and I'm not willing to go against God's desires or promises. Envy will rob you of your life and sometimes your mind. It is a thief that steals your God-given talents. How can you grow your talents when you are sitting back watching others' success and not building your own? I pray that I will always be satisfied with God's blessings and the talents he bestowed on me. I refuse to allow being envious of others to destroy me.

SOMETHING TO THINK ABOUT

Is there a difference between jealousy and envious? If so, describe the difference. Do you fall into either category?

_____

_____

_____

_____

_____

Do you think others are better or more successful than you are?

_____

_____

_____

_____

_____

Do you celebrate the success of others, or wish their downfall?

_____

_____

_____

_____

_____

How can you be satisfied with God's blessings?

TODAY'S ASSIGNMENT

Do you know someone who has written a book, made a CD of their music, made a candle, or completed a project they have worked on? Pick up the phone and call them to congratulate them on their success. Let someone know today that you are excited about their blessings and that you will support them. Call or send a postcard. Acknowledge someone during the rest of the week for their achievement(s) or completion of a project.

_____

_____

_____

_____

_____

_____

_____

_____

_____

_____

_____

_____

DAY 27

Matthew 7:7

Ask, and it shall be given you; seek, and ye shall find; knock, and it shall be opened unto you.

FALLING IN LOVE WITH JESUS

In 2003 I walked out of my home to walk our tiny little Pekinese dog who we loved. As I walked out of my yard, the neighbor's huge bulldog chased us back into our yard. He was mean and had once again broken out of his owner's fenced in back yard. When I saw the dog, he began to bark profusely and run toward us. I grabbed our dog into my arms and ran as fast as I could in high-heeled boots. I tripped on the concrete steps, still holding onto my dog for dear life. I crawled to the door, reached up, and opened it, tossing our dog inside the house. Next, I slammed the door shut. My ankle was aching, but I managed to turn around to face the big dog. I had slammed the door closed with my back pushed against it. I screamed at the bulldog staring at me, preparing to attack. Through tears, I told the dog to get away. When he didn't, I called on Jesus. The mean animal sauntered away. After days in pain, I had to go to the emergency room and found that my ankle was sprained.

Since that day I have fallen several times. Each time, injuring my knees. Each time calling on the blood of Jesus. Each time, I survived the fall. Once I had knee surgery after walking around with excruciating pain, having seen several doctors, and getting x-rays. I eventually complained to the insurance company about my doctors. I felt the doctors I had seen were not doing the best to diagnose my pain. They sent me to a specialist who ordered an MRI, which located the problem. I had torn ligaments deep in the back of my knee that x-rays could not find. The doctor said he didn't know how I had continued to work and wear heels with that much pain. I knew God had blessed me.

After the dog issue, I had fallen maybe four times, each one being worse. Each fall I called on Jesus to save me. He stopped me from slamming my head into my car after falling out of my garage door and missing all the steps. Instead of hitting my head on the car's bumper, I fell next to it, still on concrete pavement. There was another time I slid on slippery floors in my socks while chasing our dog. I hit my head on the bottom of the kitchen stove. Jesus saved me again.

Another horrible fall sent me to the emergency room where I was diagnosed with one of the worse shoulder dislocations the attending doctor had seen. They had to put me to sleep to reset it. Still, I knew God had carried me. I was in so much pain that all I could do was cry.

How could I not love God when every time I needed him, He was there, and when I called Him, He answered? When I asked, He provided. After every stumble, God protected me. My love for Him increased every single time. In Matthew 7:7, it reads: Ask, and it shall be given you; seek, and ye shall find; knock, and it shall be opened unto you. My experience with this verse and with God responding is that He does not make promises He doesn't keep. Every time I fell, I asked him to save me, and He did. In my life, I am a witness that God is not a liar. When He makes a promise, He keeps it. Every day I fall more in love with God.

SOMETHING TO THINK ABOUT

Can you recall a time you had to call on Jesus and He responded? What happened?

_____

_____

_____

_____

_____

Did he respond to your request? If He did not, how did you feel?

_____

_____

_____

_____

Has there been a time in your life, that you didn't call on God, but He still helped you?

_____

_____

_____

_____

_____

Have you fallen in love with Jesus? If not, there are several things you can do to help. You can read your Bible and pray for understanding. Attend Bible classes and learn as much as you can about Jesus. Pray and ask God for help to understand. Are you willing to fall in love with Jesus?

_____

_____

_____

_____

_____

ASSIGNMENT FOR TODAY

Read Matthew 7:7 and think about a time in your life when you asked God for something. Have a discussion with a friend who is on a Christian journey about this Bible verse. What has been their experience? Research and dig deep into your heart to see a time in your life when God helped you. Ask God to direct your steps as you research in your life the possibilities of God responding to your needs.

_____

_____

_____

_____

_____

_____

_____

_____

_____

_____

_____

_____

_____

DAY 28

Exodus 20:8

Remember the sabbath day, to keep it holy.

THE TRUTH SHALL SET YOU FREE

I was thirteen when my mom's best friend told my mom she was a Seventh Day Adventist. Mom and her best friend had been members of the same church for years. They were solid Baptist Christians and worked in the church. Both were singers, ushers, choir members, and taught Sunday School. So, when her friend visited a tent revival that arrived in East St. Louis, Illinois, she enjoyed it, did her research, and left the Baptist church where her husband was an associate minister. This Christian woman left her home church, where her husband and family were respected members, and her husband was a regular speaker on the pastor's preaching rotation list.

My mother was shocked. When her friend began to teach her about the Sabbath being Saturday, my mom sought advice and did her research to find the truth. I remember my mom telling us all about the Sabbath and what we should not be doing on the day God had set aside for us to rest. But even though she shared that information with us, she told us she was on the search for Biblical truth.

My mother went to about four pastors and asked them if the Sabbath was on Saturday. Three of the pastors told her it was not. The fourth one kept telling her to come back, but he would not be there every time she went. Finally, she saw him running out of the building and jumping in his car to leave when his staff told him she had returned. On that day, my mother decided it might be some truth to the Sabbath being honored on Saturday. So, like her friend, when the tent arrived the following year, Mom went and took six of her eight children with her.

I enjoyed the service, the singing, and the preaching. But some of the information being taught from Revelations was downright scary. Mom continued to take us. I met new friends and enjoyed the local church hosting the revival. Then it happened—Mom went up to be baptized. Later that year, after she joined the church, six of her kids, including me, gave our lives to Christ and were baptized into the Seventh Day Adventist denomination.

As teenagers, it was hard for me to not participate in school activities that were being held on Friday nights. For a long time, I never told my friends why I couldn't go out with them on Friday nights. Eventually, I started following the crowd, and though Mom didn't like it, she continued to pray for me and asked God to help me to honor the Sabbath. Finally, mom came up with a plan. She began to have Sabbath activities on Friday nights. We would sing, pray, and read the Bible, and Mom would tell us stories. We learned that if God says to do something, you did it, if you wanted to have everlasting life. We learned that God said to remember the Sabbath and to keep it holy. He didn't tell us to remember it because he wanted to change it or for us to forget it. I learned through Biblical teachings, my church, and my mom, that God does not lie or change his mind. If he said to remember the Sabbath, which is Saturday, we should understand that the Sabbath is important to Him. The Sabbath is Saturday, and that, too, is something we should never forget.

SOMETHING TO THINK ABOUT

What day do you celebrate the Sabbath?
___
___
___
___
___

How do you think the Sabbath changed from Saturday to Sunday?
___
___
___
___
___

Do you think God changed the Sabbath when He asked us to *remember the Sabbath*?
___
___
___
___

What is stopping you from doing what God asks you to do in relationship to the Sabbath?

_____

_____

_____

_____

_____

ASSIGNMENT FOR TODAY

Find out where the Bible talks about the Sabbath and read it for a better understanding. The Bible speaks about the Sabbath being the seventh day of the week. Research in the dictionary, encyclopedia or on Google to find out what is the seventh day of the week. If you want to know why your church celebrates the Sabbath on a Sunday, talk to your pastor.

_____

_____

_____

_____

_____

_____

_____

_____

_____

_____

_____

_____

_____

DAY 29

Isaiah 40:31

But they that wait upon the Lord shall renew their strength; they shall mount up with wings as eagles; they shall run, and not be weary; they shall walk, and not faint.

WAITING ON GOD

Have you ever asked God for something and you waited and waited, but nothing happened? How did you feel? Did you lose faith and decide that God couldn't hear you, or that He refused to answer your prayers?

This has happened to a lot of people. We ask God to bless us, and when he fails to do so, we either feel let down, stop believing, or lose trust in what the Bible teaches us.

I remember times when I asked God for something and didn't receive it. I recalled crying on my mom's shoulders and asking her why God didn't answer my prayers. Was I not worthy? Did God not love me? I watched others get the things they prayed for, and yet God seemed to ignore my personal requests.

What my mother told me was that we cannot hurry God. She further explained that God comes in His own timing, or she would say something like, "God's timing is not like ours." She said what I was asking for may not be in my best interest, and God knew what I needed. She assured me that what I was asking for was much less than what God had planned for my life, but if I would wait and not become weary, God would answer and show me what His plans were for my life. Years later, I understood.

I will give you an example. When I was about ten years old, I knew what I wanted as an adult. I wanted a husband, a Volkswagen, and a son. I prayed for that because I knew I was not going to want to date around. It was not for me. As an adult, I wasn't going to be sitting around waiting. I trusted God for what I was asking. Deep inside, I knew whatever God had planned would be greater. As I turned down dates, I became more patient, less weary, and knew that I would not suffer because God had me. As expected, I met my husband. Like Mom said, His plan for me was greater. I could not imagine my life being better. That Volkswagen became a 4-door Volvo, and the son, a daughter. God also blessed us with a home we had built. As we grew in our relationship, God's plan for our lives included financial freedom to help others. I could not imagine His greater for me.

I'm so glad I didn't give up. I am glad I waited on Him while becoming stronger. I didn't faint or doubt Him.

SOMETHING TO THINK ABOUT

Has there ever been a time in your life when you prayed for something, and it didn't happen?

_____
_____
_____
_____
_____

How did you feel when God didn't deliver as you asked?

_____
_____
_____
_____
_____

Did you give up, or did you wait?

_____
_____
_____
_____

Each of us may interpret this Bible verse differently. (Isaiah 40:31) What does it mean to you?

_____

_____

_____

_____

_____

How long do you wait on God for your blessings?

_____

_____

_____

_____

_____

ASSIGNMENT FOR TODAY

Think about a prayer request you asked for. Did you get it or was the blessing you received greater? Share your testimony today with someone who is struggling to have faith. Help them to not give up or faint. Talk to them about renewing their faith and how to strengthen their walk with God. Let them know that sometimes God's plans for our lives are better than the requests we make. Pray with them. Encourage them to mount up their wings, to work on their desires, and to have patience with God.

DAY 30

Psalms 100:4

Enter into his gates with thanksgiving, and into his courts with praise: be thankful unto him, and bless his name.

THANKFUL AND BLESSED

I have been super blessed for most of my life. When I was young, I thought we were rich because whatever I asked my mom or dad for I usually received. By now, you know my mom was a praying woman who taught us to pray and to be thankful. For years, I watched her keep a beautiful home and cars, yet Mom never worked. My father was the bread winner. He worked two jobs to take care of his family of ten, including himself. None of my siblings or I knew this about our father. We only knew he had a full-time job and a small business working on cars. We had no clue that he was also a welder, until much later.

Our family's blessings ran deep. Because of that, my mother didn't mind helping others. There were times I would get angry because she would buy clothing, pay bills, and buy food for others when needed. I believed she was too free-hearted, and folks were taking advantage of her and my father. My mother would always say, "To whom much is given, much is expected." Still, I didn't understand anything about what she was saying. I knew my family was blessed, but still I wanted things.

As I grew older, I understood what my mom meant. I remember, as a first grader, sharing my money or food with others. I don't know why I did it; I guess because I saw my momma do it. Mother continued to help others. The more she helped, the more it seemed others came. She didn't give folks things on a whim, but if she knew someone needed it, she would help.

Mother told me when you help others in need, God will give you double portions. Now that I am a woman, I realize I am my mother. I have so much, and I don't mind sharing it with someone who needs the support. I have taken care of the needs or wants of many people, but I still long to accomplish my dreams.

I am an avid Facebook fan. I post lots of statuses on everything. I use social media as my personal marketing billboard. It has been useful in helping me find friends and relatives. It can also allow many of us to showcase our skills, abilities, and successes. However, if you are not careful, it can make you envious, jealous and unsure of yourself and your talents.

On social media it appears as if everyone is successful and God is sending blessings from every direction. Then you begin to think, why won't God answer my prayers for blessings? Does he not hear my prayers? Does He even care? You see all these posts about, "how I made a million," people getting movie deals, books going straight to the New York bestsellers status, and all these coaching entrepreneurs bragging about the number of clients they have and their success. They model their designer bags and clothes. It can make you feel left out.

One day I asked God a question because He is my father and I should be able to come to him with my questions and/or concerns. I said, "God where is mine? I want to become a popular New York bestseller. I want the expensive purses and cars."

As I continued, I received a call from a friend. I asked, "What do you think God's call is for my life?" She told me to pray and listen for God's answer. I prayed, but it took too long for God to respond. I believe God didn't hear me, or I couldn't identify his voice. I had been told He would talk to me, but I needed to be able to hear him speak.

The next night, I dreamed about a lot of things. In one I dreamed I was praying. God had blessed me with exactly what I already have. The next morning, it occurred to me that God had given me and my husband so much that I had been able to bless more than 40 others in many kind deeds. I immediately wrote in my journal. "Why am I searching and burning the midnight candle and all this steam?" I thought I was doing it to get the things these folks on Facebook were constantly bragging about. I wrote something like this in my journal, "Why are you hustling and grinding so much like others when you already have what they are trying to get?"

It hit me like a ton of filled water bottles falling off a shelf, hitting me everywhere on my body. You are right, God. You have already given me what most people want. I live in a 4,000 square foot home that was paid off on the signing day. You have blessed us with beautiful cars that most would say are expensive. I haven't had any major bills outside of utility bills. I looked around at my new furniture that we paid for in cash. I could quit work now and not have to worry. Everything many of the Facebookers say they are hustling to get, I already have, and more. I stopped hustling at that moment because my heavenly father had answered my prayers. However, because I was like a fish who had never been out of water, I didn't realize I had more than enough. It didn't reach my empty mind that I was blessed beyond my needs. That was the day I wrote my resignation letter to retire. God blessed me. When I am not looking at others, I see all the things He's done for me and for my family.

SOMETHING TO THINK ABOUT

What did you want to be when you grew up?
_____
_____
_____
_____
_____

Did your desires change?
_____
_____
_____
_____
_____

Do you feel that you have accomplished all your dreams?
_____
_____
_____
_____
_____

What role has God played in your accomplishments?

___

Are you influenced by others who claim they are successful but never mention God in their testimony?

___

What have you asked God to do for you?

___

Has He done it?

_____
_____
_____
_____
_____

Do you feel rejected and/or neglected if you have not heard from our Father in Heaven?

_____
_____
_____
_____
_____

What can you do to receive a blessing on your life from God?

_____
_____
_____
_____
_____

TODAY'S ASSIGNMENT

Get a pencil and paper. Take an inventory of your skills and abilities. Think about what you are good at and write down what skills you do well. Think about your prayer life and how often you speak to God. Write down your goals and dreams.

_____

_____

_____

_____

_____

_____

_____

_____

_____

_____

_____

_____

_____

_____

_____

FINAL WORDS

I wanted to write this devotion to not only help others but to help *me*. My entire life I have been taught about God, about His love for us, and how we should always honor Him. The thing that I remember the most is that God loves us so much that He gave His only son to save us from sin. Yet, often we don't trust Him with our most desired hopes, dreams, and lives. My mother worked hard to teach us to lean on God and to trust Him.

As I stated, I have been going to church my entire life. From Mom's early childhood until she became bedridden, she continued to attend church. Though she could no longer sing in the choir, usher and be a deaconess, she still supported the departments with her presence. Mom took us to church and encouraged us to participate in all the available activities. Until this day, I am still in church and taking part in many activities.

My most visual memories are of my siblings and I saying Easter speeches, singing in church, going to Sunday School, then to Sabbath School.

Even as a young child, I knew we were expected to worship God and to go to church whether Mom was in the city or not. Almost fifty-seven years later, I still hate missing church.

The hardest part of my salvation has been learning to do all the things I was expected to do, like study the Bible, pray, and keep the Sabbath. Growing up as Methodist and Baptist, I attended church on Sunday. When we learned about the Sabbath, we changed over to attending church on Saturday. As children, it was hard. Though we loved God, we loved our friends and television. All of that was supposed to stop because we had found that the Sabbath was Saturday. We had to keep the Sabbath from sundown Friday to sundown Saturday. It was challenging in high school and college, and even today.

Following the Ten Commandments for me was easy, except for one: *Remember the Sabbath day; to keep it holy* is important to me. I pray for God to help me constantly with this commandment. I am not perfect. I try hard. It is my prayer that God will continue to help me. He has answered most of my prayers, and I know He will continue to help me, and all the readers of this devotion, as we work hard to do His will.

Writing this devotion book has been a blessing for me. I was able to look into my past, remember my loving mother who gave her life to God at nine years old, and who strived to live her life for God. Though she was not perfect, she loved the Lord with all her might. She loved Him so much that she dedicated all her children's lives to Him and made sure we knew that we could always call on Him when we were in trouble. I am thankful for what she has given us. What my mom gave us is far better than silver, gold, or other material things. She gave us Jesus. She taught us that with Him, we could become or be anything we wanted in life. All we needed to do was keep Him first.

It is not my intention to brag, but I have learned that there are more ways to bring people to God. We bring them to Him through our experiences, our love, our actions, and by showing folks that with God all is possible. The Bible says, in 1 Chronicles 16:8: "Give thanks unto the LORD, call upon his name, make known his deeds among the people." What that says to me is that as God blesses us, our instructions are to share those blessings with others, to teach them about God, and what God can do for us when we honor Him.

I am so glad I know Him. I want you to know through my words, the road I traveled to get to this point, what my experiences were with my family, church, and God. Another thing I wanted to share is that it is important for parents to teach their children about God. They should teach their children how to read the Bible and pray. I am thankful my grandparents taught my mom. I am thankful my mom passed it down to us, and I have passed it to my child.

I love God. I want the world to know He is good. He is great. He is merciful, and He loves you and me. Give Him a try!

May God bless every reader of this devotion.

Rose

DEDICATION

This book is dedicated to the late Deborah Harrison and Kimberly Hawkins. Deb, I miss you dearly. Kim, I appreciate you so much for your encouragement and let's continue to talk often.